T0156050

Communications in Computer and Information Science 1271

Commenced Publication in 2007
Founding and Former Series Editors:
Simone Diniz Junqueira Barbosa, Phoebe Chen, Alfredo Cuzzocrea,
Xiaoyong Du, Orhun Kara, Ting Liu, Krishna M. Sivalingam,
Dominik Ślęzak, Takashi Washio, Xiaokang Yang, and Junsong Yuan

Editorial Board Members

More information about this series at http://www.springer.com/series/7899

Gang Wang · Arridhana Ciptadi ·
Ali Ahmadzadeh (Eds.)

Deployable Machine Learning for Security Defense

First International Workshop, MLHat 2020
San Diego, CA, USA, August 24, 2020
Proceedings

 Springer

Editors
Gang Wang 🄳
University of Illinois at Urbana Champaign
Urbana, IL, USA

Arridhana Ciptadi
Blue Hexagon Inc.
Sunnyvale, CA, USA

Ali Ahmadzadeh
Blue Hexagon Inc.
Sunnyvale, CA, USA

ISSN 1865-0929 ISSN 1865-0937 (electronic)
Communications in Computer and Information Science
ISBN 978-3-030-59620-0 ISBN 978-3-030-59621-7 (eBook)
https://doi.org/10.1007/978-3-030-59621-7

This Springer imprint is published by the registered company Springer Nature Switzerland AG
The registered company address is: Gewerbestrasse 11, 6330 Cham, Switzerland

Preface

In recent years, we have seen machine learning algorithms, particularly deep learning algorithms, revolutionizing many domains such as computer vision, speech, and natural language processing. In contrast, the impact of these new advances in machine learning is still fairly limited in the domain of security defense. While there is research progress in applying machine learning for threat forensics, malware analysis, intrusion detection, and vulnerability discovery, there are still grand challenges to be addressed before a machine learning system can be deployed and operated in practice as a critical component of cyber defense. Major challenges include, but are not limited to, the scale of the problem (billions of known attacks), adaptability (hundreds of millions of new attacks every year), inference speed and efficiency (compute resource is constrained), adversarial attacks (highly motivated evasion and poisoning attacks), the surging demand for explainability (for threat investigation), and the need for integrating human (e.g., SOC analysts) in the loop.

To address these challenges, we hosted the First International Workshop on Deployable Machine Learning for Security Defense (MLHat 2020). The workshop was collocated with 25th ACM SIGKDD Conference on Knowledge Discovery and Data Mining (KDD 2020). This workshop brought together academic researchers and industry practitioners to discuss the open challenges, potential solutions, and best practices to deploy machine learning at scale for security defense. The goal was to define new machine learning paradigms under various security application contexts, identifying exciting new future research directions. At the same time, the workshop had a strong industry presence to provide insights into the challenges of deploying and maintaining machine learning models, and the much-needed discussion on the capabilities that the state of the arts failed to provide.

In total, the workshop received 13 submissions as novel research papers. All of the submissions were peer reviewed in a single-blind manner. Each submission received three reviews from the Program Committee members. 8 papers were accepted (as full papers) and presented during the workshop.

August 2020

Gang Wang
Arridhana Ciptadi
Ali Ahmadzadeh

Organization

Organizing and Program Committee Chairs

Gang Wang	University of Illinois at Urbana-Champaign, USA
Arridhana Ciptadi	Blue Hexagon, USA
Ali Ahmadzadeh	Blue Hexagon, USA

Program Committee

Sadia Afroz	Avast, USA
Shang-Tse Chen	National Taiwan University, Taiwan
Yin Chen	Google, USA
Neil Gong	Duke University, USA
Zhou Li	University of California, Irvine, USA
Shirin Nilizadeh	The University of Texas at Arlington, USA
B. Aditya Prakash	Georgia Tech, USA
Gianluca Stringhini	Boston University, USA
Ting Wang	Penn State University, USA
Xinyu Xing	Penn State University, USA

Contents

Understanding the Adversaries

A Large-Scale Analysis of Attacker Activity in Compromised Enterprise Accounts

Neil Shah[1,2]([⊠]), Grant Ho[1,2], Marco Schweighauser[2], Mohamed Ibrahim[2], Asaf Cidon[3], and David Wagner[1]

[1] UC Berkeley, Berkeley, CA 94720, USA
`neilshah430@berkeley.edu`
[2] Barracuda Networks, Campbell, CA 95008, USA
[3] Columbia University, New York, NY 10027, USA

Abstract. We present a large-scale characterization of attacker activity across 111 real-world enterprise organizations. We develop a novel forensic technique for distinguishing between attacker activity and benign activity in compromised enterprise accounts that yields few false positives and enables us to perform fine-grained analysis of attacker behavior. Applying our methods to a set of 159 compromised enterprise accounts, we quantify the duration of time attackers are active in accounts and examine thematic patterns in how attackers access and leverage these hijacked accounts. We find that attackers frequently dwell in accounts for multiple days to weeks, suggesting that delayed (non-real-time) detection can still provide significant value. Based on an analysis of the attackers' timing patterns, we observe two distinct modalities in how attackers access compromised accounts, which could be explained by the existence of a specialized market for hijacked enterprise accounts: where one class of attackers focuses on compromising and selling account access to another class of attackers who exploit the access such hijacked accounts provide. Ultimately, our analysis sheds light on the state of enterprise account hijacking and highlights fruitful directions for a broader space of detection methods, ranging from new features that hone in on malicious account behavior to the development of non-real-time detection methods that leverage malicious activity after an attack's initial point of compromise to more accurately identify attacks.

Keywords: Compromised enterprise accounts · Characterization of attacker activity · Account hijacking

1 Introduction

With the growth of cloud-backed services and applications, ranging from email and document storage to business operations such as sales negotiations and time sheet tracking, modern enterprise accounts provide a wealth of access to

© Springer Nature Switzerland AG 2020
G. Wang et al. (Eds.): MLHat 2020, CCIS 1271, pp. 3–27, 2020.
https://doi.org/10.1007/978-3-030-59621-7_1

sensitive data and functionality. As a result, attackers have increasingly focused on compromising enterprise cloud accounts through attacks such as phishing. For example, several government agencies have issued advisories and reports warning that phishing represents "the most devastating attacks by the most sophisticated attackers" and detailing the billions of dollars in financial harmed caused by enterprise phishing and account compromise [18,31]. Not limited to financial gain, attackers have also compromised enterprise cloud accounts for personal and political motives, such as in the 2016 US presidential election, when nation-state adversaries dumped a host of internal emails from high-profile figures involved with Hillary Clinton's presidential campaign and the Democratic National Committee [38].

Given the growing importance of online accounts and credentials, a large body of existing work has focused on building mechanisms to defend against attacks through better credential hygiene, detecting phishing attacks, and stronger user authentication [14,15,20,22,23,34,37]. Despite these advances, account hijacking, the compromise and malicious use of cloud accounts, remains a widespread and costly problem [8]. Although prior work has characterized what attackers do with a hijacked account, [13,30,36], existing work focuses heavily on compromised personal email accounts. While these insights are useful, it remains unclear how well they generalize to compromised *enterprise* accounts and whether attacks on enterprise accounts have different characteristics. Unlike personal accounts, enterprise accounts often have access to a wealth of sensitive business data, and an attacker who compromises one enterprise account can use the identities of the compromised account to launch additional attacks on other employees, expanding their access to other data and assets within the enterprise.

To close this knowledge gap and identify additional avenues for defending enterprise accounts, we conduct a large-scale analysis of attacker activity within compromised enterprise accounts. We analyze a historical dataset of nearly 160 real-world compromise accounts from over 100 organizations that have been confirmed as compromised by both a commercial security product (Barracuda Networks) and by the organization's IT or security team. First, given a compromised account, we develop a method that allows us to identify what account actions correspond to activity by the attacker versus the benign user. Evaluating our approach on a random sample of enterprise accounts, we find that our forensic technique yields a false positive rate of 11% and a precision of 94%.

Using this method for fine-grained attacker behavior analysis, we find that for over one-third of the hijacked accounts in our dataset, the attacker's activity occurs across a week or more. This extended dwell time suggests that there is value in developing (non-real-time) detection techniques that analyze account behavior over longer time horizons to more accurately identify compromise and mitigate an attack before its completed execution. Additionally, based on a deeper analysis of the access timing patterns within these accounts, we identify two different modes in the way attackers utilize hijacked accounts. In particular, the access patterns of hijacked accounts with long durations of attacker activity could reflect the existence of a specialized market of account compromise, where one set of attackers focuses on compromising enterprise accounts and subsequently sells account access to another set of attackers who focus on utilizing the hijacked account.

Finally, examining the kinds of data and applications that attackers access via these enterprise accounts, we find that most attackers in our dataset do not access many applications outside of email, which suggests that either many enterprise cloud accounts do not have access to interesting data and functionality outside of email, or that attackers have yet to adapt to and exploit these additional resources.

2   Data

Our work starts with a historical dataset consisting of 989 compromised enterprise accounts from 120 real-world organizations. We rely on two pieces of information for ground-truth labeling. First, all of these organizations use a commercial anti-fraud service (Barracuda Sentinel) for preventing phishing and account takeover attacks [2,14]. For each of the compromised accounts in our dataset, Barracuda's detectors flagged at least one event (e.g., a user login or a user-sent email) as malicious. Additionally, all of these compromised instances were verified by their organization's IT or security team. For the remainder of the paper, we will use the terms *compromised enterprise account, compromised user, compromised account,* and *account* interchangeably.

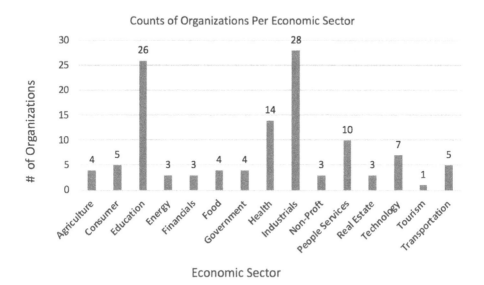

Fig. 1. Categorization of the 120 organizations in our dataset across various economic sectors.

Figure 1 shows the distribution of the 120 organizations by economic sector. A majority of these organizations belong to the industrials, education, health, and people services economic sectors, with counts of 28, 26, 14, and 10 respectively. These four sectors represent 65% of the set of organizations in our dataset.

2.1   Schema and Data Sources

Our dataset consists of Microsoft Office 365 cloud audit log events [3,6] for all of the compromised accounts we study. Each time a user logs into their account, accesses an Office 365 application (e.g., Outlook, Sharepoint, and Excel), or performs an account operation (e.g., a password reset), Office 365 records an audit log event. Across the 989 compromised accounts, our dataset consists of 927,822 audit log events from August 1, 2019–January 27, 2020, where each account was marked as compromised during that time window. At a high level, each audit event in our logs includes the following key fields:

- Id - Unique identifier for an audit event
- UserId - Email of user who performed the operation
- UserAgent - Identifier string of device that performed the operation
- ClientIp - IP address of the device that performed the operation
- Operation - Operation performed by the user
- ApplicationId - Id of Office 365 application acted upon

The Operation field indicates which cloud operation the user performed, such as a successful user login or a password reset. Note that based on the way Office 365 generates these audit events, only events that reflect an account login or application access contain values for UserAgent and ClientIp; audit events for other operations (such as a password reset event) don't contain user agent or IP address information. Throughout the paper, we will refer to the audit events that are login or application accesses as "application login events" or "login events". We also augment the information above by using MaxMind [28] to identify the country and country subdivision (e.g, state or province) of each available Client IP address.

Additionally, we draw upon several other data sources to help evaluate our technique for distinguishing between benign versus attacker activity within a compromised account (evaluation procedure detailed in Appendix A.2 of our extended technical report [33]): the raw emails sent by users in our dataset and any audit events, emails [4], and inbox forwarding rules flagged by Barracuda's machine learning detectors for the compromised users.

As we discuss in Sect. 3.2, in order to prevent a large batch of compromised accounts from a single attacker or organization from skewing our analysis results, we de-duplicate this set of 989 compromised accounts to a final dataset of 159 compromised accounts across 111 organizations.

2.2   Ethics

This work reflects a collaboration between researchers at UC Berkeley, Columbia University, and a large security company, Barracuda Networks. The set of organizations included in our dataset are customers of Barracuda, and is secured using standard industry best practices.

Due to the confidential nature of account data, only authorized employees of Barracuda Networks accessed the data, and no sensitive data was released to anyone outside of Barracuda Networks. Our project received approval from Barracuda Networks, and strong security controls were implemented to ensure confidentiality and limited scope of access.

3   Detecting Attacker Activity

Compromised accounts contain a mix of activity, such as application accesses (logins), from both the true user and an attacker. In order to accurately analyze attacker usage of hijacked accounts, we developed a ruleset, based on well-known anomaly detection ideas [10, 32], for identifying which audit events correspond to activity from the attacker versus a benign user.

Throughout this section, when describing the components of our rule set, we use the name Bob to refer to a generic compromised user from our dataset. Our rule set first builds a historical profile for Bob that represents the typical locations and user agent strings that he uses to log into his account. We then use this profile to classify future login events as either attacker-related or benign by identifying actions that deviate from the historical profile. Our rule set is not guaranteed to find every attack, nor does it guarantee robustness against motivated attackers trying to evade detection. However our rule set is still relatively comprehensive and generates few false positives.

3.1   Historical User Profile and Features

Historical User Profile. Conceptually, a user's historical profile reflects the typical activity (operations, login provenance, etc.) that the user makes under benign circumstances. To construct this profile, we assume that historical login events that occurred significantly (one month) before any known compromise activity reflect benign behavior by the true user. For each compromised user (Bob), we find the earliest time, t, that any of Barracuda's detectors flagged the account as compromised. To create Bob's historical user profile, we first retrieve a set of historical login events from the time window of 2 months prior to t until 1 month prior to t (i.e., one-month of historical data). From this historical dataset, we construct a historical profile for Bob that consists of 3 sets of values: the set of country subdivisions (states or provinces) that he logged in from during that time period, the set of countries he has logged in from, and the set of user agents that he has logged in with.

Features. Given a recent event, e, that we wish to classify as malicious or benign activity, we extract 2 features based on a user's historical profile. First, we extract a numerical geolocation feature by comparing the geolocation of e's IP address to the set of geolocations in the user's historical profile:

(a) If e represents a login from a country that was never seen in Bob's historical user profile, then assign e's geolocation feature value a **2** (most suspicious).

(b) Otherwise, if e represent a login from a country subdivision not found in Bob's historical user profile, then assign e's geolocation feature value a **1** (medium suspicion).

(c) Otherwise, assign e's geolocation feature value a **0** (least suspicious).

We also extract a user agent feature that captures the suspiciousness of the user agent of e. All user agents are normalized in a pre-processing step: the version number is removed and only the device and model identifiers are retained, so a user agent string such as `iPhone9C4/1706.56` is normalized to `iPhone9C4`. Thus, `iPhone9C4/1706.56` and `iPhone9C4/1708.57` yield the same normalized user agent. The user agent feature is then defined as follows:

(a) If e's normalized user agent does not match any of the normalized user agents in Bob's historical user profile, then assign e's user agent feature value a **1** (most suspicious).

(b) Otherwise, assign e's user agent feature value a **0** (least suspicious).

3.2   Classification Rule Set

In order to identify the set of attacker actions within a compromised account, we start by selecting the first known compromise event that Barracuda's detectors marked as malicious and that was confirmed by the organization's IT team. Next, we compute a user's historical profile as described above and use it to extract features for every login event in a two-month window centered around this first confirmed compromise event (i.e., all login events in the month preceding this initial compromise time as well as all login events in the one month following the initial compromise time). We then apply the following set of rules to classify the login events in this "recent" two-month window as attacker activity or not. Below, we present a high-level sketch of our rule set and discuss assumptions made in the development of our rules. We defer further details and evaluation results to Sect. 3.2 and Appendix A.2 of our extended technical report [33].

Rules. For a compromised account (Bob), each recent event contains a geolocation feature, denoted as **geo**, and a user agent feature, denoted as **ua**, as described above. Given these features, we mark an event as malicious or benign based on the following rule set:

```
if geo == 2
    mark e as malicious (attacker related)
else if (geo == 1) and (ua == 1)
    mark e as malicious
else
    mark e as benign
```

Intuition and Assumptions. The geolocation and user agent features quantify the suspiciousness of a new login event in relation to a user's historical profile.

We assume that the historical login events for each user do not contain attacker activity; i.e., that the attacker has not operated within the account for over one month prior to detection. However, it is possible that some of the events shortly preceding the initial confirmed compromise could be attacker related. Thus, we conservatively analyze one month's worth of events preceding a user's first confirmed compromise event to more comprehensively capture and analyze the full timeline of an attack.

Our rule set also assumes that it is less common for users to travel to another country than to another state or province within their home country. Although traveling abroad is common in some industries, we assume that most employees travel more frequently to another state or region within their residential country rather than to an entirely different country. As a result, if a login event contains an IP address mapped to a country that was never seen before in a user's historical login events, the event in question is marked as an attacker event. For travel within the same country, the country subdivision and user agent need to be new for a login event to be marked as an attacker event.

Applying Rule Set to Compromised Users. For each user Bob, we classify all login events from one month prior to t to t using a historical user profile based on events from two months prior to t to one month prior to t. Then, we classify all events from t to one month after t using a historical user profile based on events from two months prior to t to one month prior to t, and all events from one month prior to t to t that were classified as benign. Thus we update the historical user profile for each user after classifying the first month of login events [7]. Malekian et al. also describes a similar approach [27] where the historical profile is updated to reflect new patterns in user behaviors in e-commerce for the purposes of detecting online user profile-based fraud. Therefore, the last month of Bob's events are classified using an updated historical user profile that incorporates benign activity from his previous month of login events.

After applying this rule set to the 989 compromised accounts in our dataset, we identified 653 accounts (across 111 organizations) that contained at least one attack event. 276 of the 989 compromised users didn't have any historical login events due to the fact that these users' enterprises registered with Barracuda as a customer after the start of our study period, and we did not have login events from before then. As a result, our rule set couldn't be applied to these users. Of the remaining 713 users that had historical login events, 653 had at least one attacker event that our rule set classified.

We also found that 68% of the 653 compromised accounts belonged to only 6 organizations. We do not know what accounts for this skewed distribution, but it is possible that one or a few attackers specifically targeted those 6 organizations. Therefore, to ensure that our analysis results in Sect. 4 are not biased by a few attackers that compromised many accounts, we randomly sampled a subset of compromised accounts from each of the 111 organizations, resulting in a dataset of 159 compromised accounts that we use for our analysis in Sect. 4. Appendix A.1 contains more details about our sampling procedure, as well as a detailed breakdown of the 653 compromised users across the 111 organizations.

In order to evaluate the accuracy of our rule set at labeling an event as malicious or not, we randomly sampled a set of 20 compromised accounts and manually labeled each event based on the analysis procedure described in Appendix A.2 of our extended technical report [33]. Our evaluation suggests that our rule set has a false positive rate of 11% and precision of 94%.

Limitations of Rule Set and Attacker Evasion. Although our rule set has relatively high precision, we acknowledge some limitations that exist with our rules and features. Given the construction of our rule set, if a motivated attacker logs in from a state that the typical user has logged in from or with a device and model that matches that of the typical user, the attacker would successfully evade our rule set.

We did observe evidence of attackers trying to "blend in" with benign characteristics of some users, potentially to evade detection. For the 60 compromised enterprise accounts mentioned above in Sect. 3.2 in which our rule set classified no events as attacker-related, we took a random sample of 10 accounts and performed deeper analysis of the events that our rule set classified as benign. For 6 of the 10 accounts, we found that attackers only logged in from locations close in proximity to those logged in by the true user of the account (within the same states as the typical user). The geolocations appeared normal and since all 10 of these accounts were flagged by Barracuda's detectors, this is evidence of likely evasive behavior. This potentially evasive behavior parallels a result from Onaolapo et al. [30], where they found that attackers deliberately choose their geolocations to match or come close to ones used by the true user in an effort to evade detectors that look for anomalous geolocations.

For the remaining 4 accounts, we see a combination of logins from close geolocations to ones used by the true user and further geolocations (e.g. different province), but it is unclear if the logins from different provinces originate from the attacker or not given the similar user agent strings (same device and model) that are present in the event logs. This could be potential evidence for user agent masquerading, but additional work would be needed to explore this idea further.

4   Characterizing Attacker Behavior

In this section, we conduct an analysis of attacker behavior across our dataset of 159 compromised users belonging to a total of 111 organizations. Our analysis reveals three interesting aspects of modern enterprise account hijacking. First, we find that for a substantial number of accounts (51%), malicious events occur over multiple days. From a defensive standpoint, this suggests that while real-time detection is ideal, detectors that identify attacks in a delayed manner (e.g., as a result of using features based on a longer timeframe of activity) might still enable an organization to thwart an attack from achieving its goal. Second, we observe evidence that at least two distinct modes of enterprise account compromise exist. In particular, we estimate that 50% of enterprise accounts are compromised by attackers who directly leverage the information and access provided by the hijacked account. In contrast, for roughly one-third of the compromised accounts in our dataset, the attackers' access patterns suggest a compromise strategy where one set of attackers compromised the account and then sold access to the account (i.e., its credentials) to another set of actors who ultimately leveraged the account for malicious purposes (e.g., by sending spam or phishing emails). Finally, we find that attackers who compromise enterprise accounts primarily use the accounts for accessing email-related information and functionality; 78% of the hijacked accounts only accessed email applications across all their attacker events. Given that attackers did not access other applications (such as SharePoint or other corporate cloud applications), this suggests that a number of real-world attackers have not yet investigated or found value in accessing other data and functionality provided by these enterprise accounts, outside of email.

4.1   Duration of Attacker Activity and Damage Prevention

In this section, we estimate the length of time attackers are active in enterprise accounts. Our results suggest that in many cases, attackers spend multiple days exploiting the information and functionality within enterprise accounts. This suggests that even if a detector doesn't operate in a real-time fashion, it can still prevent attackers from inflicting significant damage.

Duration of Attacker Activity. Given our dataset of 159 compromised users and their respective login events, we cannot definitively determine how long an attacker compromised the account for. However, we can estimate a reasonable lower bound on the length of time an attacker is active within an account (i.e. logging in and accessing the account). For each user, we computed the difference (in seconds) between the time of the earliest attacker login event and the time of the last attacker login. As seen in Fig. 2, across all 159 compromised enterprise accounts, attackers appear to use and maintain access to many enterprise accounts for long periods of time. In almost 51% of the enterprise accounts within our dataset (81 out of 159), attackers are active for at least 1 day and in 37% of accounts, attackers are active for at least 1 week. As a result, while it's important to detect attacks in real-time, detection can still provide significant value even if it occurs after the initial compromise.

As an example of where non-real-time detection can still mitigate significant harm, we analyzed accounts that sent at least one malicious email flagged by one of Barracuda's detectors during the two month "attack window" that we applied our rule set on. Across the 11 corresponding accounts, 7 out of the 11 accounts (63%) exhibited a 3 day gap between the first malicious login event identified by our rule set and the first phishing email sent by the account (Appendix B of our extended technical report [33] shows the full interarrival distribution for all 11 accounts). In these instances, with a long gap between the initial compromise and the first phishing email, a detector that uses more computationally expensive features or detection methods, which might not be feasible to run in real-time, could prevent a significant portion of the attack activity. In the absence of such a detector, even providing manual tools for organizations to investigate whether the compromised account affected additional ones may prove beneficial.

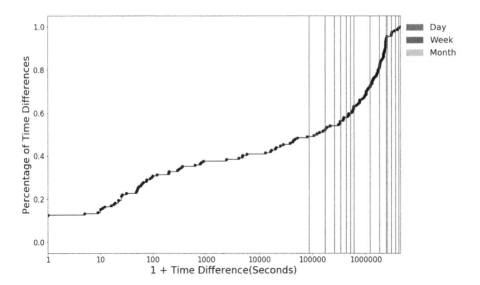

Fig. 2. The distribution of time (seconds) between the first and last attacker login event across the compromised accounts in our dataset.

4.2   Attacker Account Access Patterns

In this section, we explore the different modes in which attackers access these hijacked accounts. We estimate that in 50% of our sample of enterprise accounts, a single attacker conducts both the compromise and utilization of the account. However, for many of the remaining accounts, both the timing and application access patterns suggest that potentially two or more attackers compromise and access the hijacked account. This access pattern would be consistent with the existence of a specialized market for compromised enterprise accounts, where one set of attackers conducts the compromise and another attacker buys access to the compromised account and obtains value from the account (e.g., by accessing sensitive information or sending spam or phishing emails).

End-to-End Attackers Revisiting our findings from Sect. 4.1, we found that 81 out of 159 enterprise accounts (51%) are compromised for at least 1 day, suggesting that there are largely two main segments of compromised enterprise accounts; those that are compromised for less than a day and the remaining that appear to be compromised for a day or more. Given this preliminary result, we aim to investigate the relationship between duration of attacker activity and the economy and existence of various modes of attackers operating in the enterprise account space.

We start by investigating whether enterprise accounts are generally accessed regularly by attackers or in isolated pockets of time during the compromise lifecycle. For each of the 159 compromised enterprise accounts, we compute the interarrival time (absolute time difference) between every pair of successive attack events sorted in time. We then take the max interarrival time for each user, which represents the longest time gap between any two successive attacker accesses within an account. From Fig. 3, which shows a CDF of the max attacker interarrival times in seconds for all 159 compromised enterprise accounts, we can see that at around the 1 day mark (first red line from the left), the inflection and trend of the CDF start to change. In 53% of compromised enterprise accounts, the largest time gap between successive attacker accesses is less than 1 day, while the remaining 47% of compromised enterprise accounts (74 out of 159) have 1 or more days as their longest time gap.

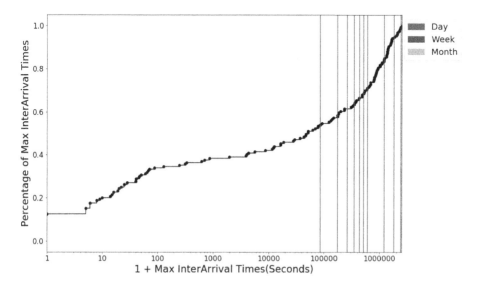

Fig. 3. Distribution of the maximum attacker interarrival times (seconds) for all 159 enterprise accounts. The maximum attacker interarrival corresponds to the longest time gap between two consecutive attack events.

A short attack life cycle (i.e., less than 1 day) seems to reflect an end-to-end compromise approach: where a single actor compromises an account and also leverages its access for further malicious actions. In our dataset, 78 out of the 159 enterprise accounts (50%) fall within this category. Due to the small time gaps between successive attacker events and relatively small durations of time attackers are active, these 78 accounts are likely compromised by a single set of attackers that both perform the compromise and use the accounts for a short period of time; it is also possible that some of these cases reflect compromise within an organization that rapidly identified and responded to the compromise incident.

Segmented Account Access. As seen in Fig. 3, 53% of enterprise accounts (74 out of 159) experienced a maximum of 1 or more days between successive attacker events. One possible explanation of the large time gap is that the initial set of attackers that compromised these accounts sold them to another set of attackers; hence, the time gaps represent the time needed for the transaction to complete. Exploring this theory, we compared attacker events before and after the max attacker interarrival time in these 74 accounts on the basis of geolocation, user agent, and internet service providers (ISPs). If the two periods of activity have significant differences across these three attributes, then that suggests that the two different activity windows could reflect access by two different sets of attackers.

To quantify the similarity of the two sets of attributes before and after the max interarrival time, we use the *Jaccard Similarity Coefficient*. Given two sets of data A and B, the Jaccard Similarity Coefficient relates the number of elements in the set intersection of A and B to the number of elements in the set union of A and B. It has been widely used in many fields [12,21,29,39] such as keyword similarity matching in search engines to test case selection for industrial software systems.

For each of the 74 compromised enterprise accounts, we gather two sets of country subdivisions mapped to attacker events before and after the max attacker interarrival time respectively. Similarly, we gather two sets of user agents and two sets of ISPs in the same manner. We then compute 3 Jaccard similarity coefficients for geolocation, user agent, and ISP respectively. In Fig. 4, most of the enterprise accounts have low Jaccard similarity coefficients for geolocation and ISP; one reason the user agent curve follows a different pattern is because of the normalization we performed, where we treat user agent strings with different device versions as the "same" underlying user agent. 50 of the enterprise accounts (around 70% of 74) had Jaccard similarity coefficients of 0.3 or less for geolocation and ISP, indicating that the sets of country subdivisions and ISPs before and after the large time gaps in these accounts were substantially different.

We also show in Appendix B.1 that if attackers are using proxy services for obtaining IP addresses, in 85% of the 74 compromised enterprise accounts, these services are fairly stable; hence, the low geolocation Jaccard similarity coefficients are not a result of attackers using unstable anonymized IP proxies or even Tor.

Given the large time gaps between successive attacker events and low similarity of the access attributes between these attack periods, we believe that 50 of the 159 enterprise accounts (31%) reflect the exploitation of a hijacked account by multiple attackers. For example, these hijacked accounts could reflect compromise that results from a specialized economy, where one set of attackers compromise the accounts and sell the account credentials to another set of attackers that specialize in monetizing or utilizing the information and access provided by the enterprise account.

In terms of understanding the potential damage inflicted by the two sets of attackers, we found that in 30 of the 50 accounts (60%), the second set of attackers that utilize the accounts access Office 365 applications at a higher rate than the first set of attackers. This further shows the importance of early mitigation in compromised enterprise accounts and that non-real-time detectors should be

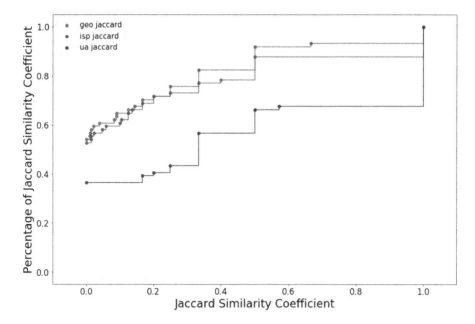

Fig. 4. Distribution of the Jaccard Similarity between Geolocation, User Agent, and ISP usage across the two time-separated attacker access periods; 74 compromised enterprise accounts had long time gaps (max interarrival times) between attacker access events.

designed to monitor continuous activity in order to prevent future damage after an account is sold. Details of our analysis are shown in Appendix B.2.

Overall, in this section, we identified two distinct patterns of compromise and access behavior that reflect attacker behavior across 81% of enterprise accounts. For many of these accounts, significant differences between the attacker's login location and access patterns suggest that modern enterprise account exploitation consists of two phases conducted by separate types of attackers: those who compromise the account and those who leverage the hijacked account's information and functionality.

4.3   Uses of Compromised Enterprise Accounts

In this section, we explore how attackers use enterprise accounts. In our dataset, attackers do not appear to establish additional access footholds into the account: they rarely change account passwords and never grant new OAuth access. In addition, within the Office 365 ecosystem, we find that attackers are not very interested in many cloud applications outside of email; 78% of the enterprise accounts only accessed email applications through attack events.

Other Operations Performed During Attacker Window. As we discussed in Sect. 2, every audit event has an `Operation` field that specifies the action that was taken. The operations we are most interested in learning if attackers perform are ones that affect a user's ability to access their account; namely, operations such as "Change user password" and "Add OAuth". The operation "Change user password" enables the user to change the password to their account, while the "Add OAuth" operation enables a user to grant applications access to certain data within their account. Since our rule set only classifies login events due to the non-empty IP and user agent fields, we gather all "Change user password" and "Add OAuth" audit events that are close in time to each account's attack events.

We find that only 2 out of 159 compromised enterprise accounts (2%) had at least one "Change user password" operation performed close in time to attacker activity. Looking deeper into the 2 accounts, we see the presence of more attacker activity after the change password operations were performed, indicating that these operations were performed by the attacker themselves. None of the 159 accounts had a single "Add OAuth" operation performed during the time period of attacker activity. Taken together, these findings suggest that attackers are not interested in changing a user's password or adding OAuth to a user's account, as this might reveal to the user that their account has been compromised and limit the amount of time the attacker can operate in the account. As a result, a "Change user password" event or "Add OAuth" event are likely not good features for detectors, as they are rarely found performed by an attacker.

Unusual Application Accesses by Attackers. We now aim to understand if there are specific Office 365 applications outside of frequently accessed email applications, such as Microsoft Exchange and Microsoft Outlook, that attackers access but the true users of the accounts don't access.

There were a total of 21 non email-related Office 365 applications that were accessed by at least one of the 159 accounts. For each of the 21 non-email applications, we determined the number of accounts that only accessed the application through their attack events and the number of accounts that only accessed the application through their benign events. The results for each of the 21 non-email applications are shown in the stacked bar chart in Fig. 5. Surprisingly, other than Ibiza Portal, none of the remaining 20 applications had the characteristic of more accounts accessing it only through attack events than number of accounts accessing it through benign events. 3 accounts accessed Ibiza Portal only through attack events, while only one account accessed it solely through benign events. Ibiza Portal, or Microsoft Azure portal, [5] enables users to build and monitor their enterprise's web and cloud applications in a simple, unified place; therefore, it might allow an attacker to view confidential data within an enterprise's applications, but retrieving that data may take longer compared to other file-sharing applications, such as Microsoft SharePoint or Microsoft Forms. In addition, Microsoft Azure Portal is very rarely accessed by true users of enterprise accounts (only one account ever accessed Microsoft Azure Portal during their benign events). Therefore, based on our dataset of compromised enterprise accounts, it does not appear that attackers are accessing cloud-based applications that typical users don't access within the Office 365 ecosystem.

Therefore, in the current state, building features for detectors around atypical accesses to cloud-based applications may not aid much in detecting attacker activity post-compromise. Future work would involve exploring additional cloud-based applications outside of Office 365.

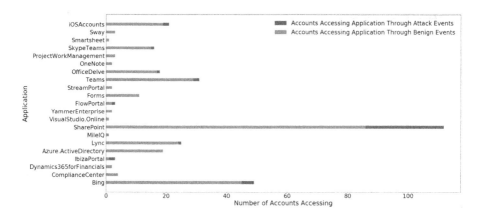

Fig. 5. Bar chart comparing number of accounts accessing each of the 21 non-email applications via only attacker-labeled events and number of accounts accessing non-email applications via only benign events from August 1, 2019–January 27, 2020.

Applications that Attackers Commonly Use. In this section, we aim to understand the types of cloud applications that attackers exploit in enterprise accounts, regardless of how common the application is for enterprises to use.

Most attackers favor email-related applications. We found that in 98% of compromised enterprise accounts (156 out of 159), attackers accessed at least one email-related Office 365 application. Much of the previous work in understanding compromised personal accounts found that attackers tended to go through user's inboxes and send phishing emails; we now see that at scale, attackers seem to be exhibiting similar behavior in enterprise accounts. We also found that in 78% of compromised enterprise accounts (124 out of 159), attackers only accessed email-related Office 365 applications. We speculate that this may be because examining a user's inbox is sufficient for attackers who want to learn more about the user and the enterprise the account belongs to.

In terms of non-email-related Office 365 applications, Microsoft Sharepoint has the highest percentage of accounts that access it through attack events (17%), with Bing as the second highest percentage at 3%. A full bar chart showing the percentage of enterprise accounts that access each non-email related Office 365 application through attack events is shown in Appendix D of our extended technical report [33]. Given the wide range of Office 365 cloud applications accessible by attackers and the abundance of information these applications harbor, it is surprising that attackers don't access these applications more often. Attackers of enterprise accounts still generally favor email-related applications, such as Microsoft Outlook, which offer a quick and convenient way for an attacker to gain access to contact lists and learn about any confidential and financial information tied to the employee and or enterprise.

5   Related Work

In this section, we highlight previous works that study detection and characterization of compromised accounts. We also draw comparisons between our findings in the space of compromised enterprise accounts and that of previous work.

5.1   Overview of Previous Work

Detection and Forensics. There has been an extensive amount of literature proposing various techniques from machine learning and anomaly detection for detecting phishing attacks in personal and enterprise accounts on a smaller scale [9,11,19,24] and on a large scale [14,22,23,34]. In addition, a limited amount of prior work exists on detecting compromised accounts [16,26] through the use of honeypot accounts and personal accounts on social networks.

Liu et al. in [26] monitored the dangers of private file leakage in P2P file-sharing networks through the use of honeyfiles containing forged private information. Their work focused more on the use of honeyfiles instead of account credentials and doesn't study compromised accounts outside of P2P.

Egele et al. in [16] developed a system, called COMPA, for detecting compromised personal accounts in social networks. COMPA constructs behavior profiles for each account and evaluates new messages posted by these social networking accounts by comparing features such as time of day and message text to the behavioral profiles. They measured a false positive rate of 4% on a large-scale dataset from Twitter and Facebook. However, their work only studies how to detect compromised personal accounts and doesn't include enterprise accounts.

As a result, none of the works in the literature have performed analysis to understand attacker activity in enterprise accounts post-compromise. Our work addresses this gap by presenting a forensic technique that allows an analyst or organization to distinguish between attacker and benign activity in enterprise accounts.

Characterization. Although there has been prior work on understanding attacker behavior and patterns within compromised accounts [13,17,30,35], most of this research has been primarily focused on understanding the nature of compromised personal accounts; few efforts have been examined the behavior of attackers in compromised enterprise accounts at large scale.

TimeKeeper, proposed by Fairbanks et al. [17], explored the characteristics of the file system in honeypot accounts controlled by attackers. Although their work applied forensic techniques to honeypot accounts post-compromise, they operated at small scale and only characterized attacker behavior in relation to file systems on these accounts.

Onaolapo et al. [30] studied attacker behavior in small-scale hijacked Gmail accounts post-compromise and characterized attacker activity based on where the account credentials were leaked. They also devised a taxonomy of attacker activity accessing the Gmail accounts, noting the presence of four attacker types (curious, gold diggers, spammers, and hijackers). However, their work did not examine compromised enterprise accounts and they were only able to monitor certain actions, such as opening an email or creating a draft of an email.

Bursztein et al. [13] examined targeted account compromise through the use of various data sources, such as phishing pages targeting Google users and high-confidence hijacked Google accounts. However, their work focuses on compromised personal accounts and not on enterprise accounts.

5.2   Comparing Enterprise Versus Personal Account Hijacking

Duration of Attacker Activity. Extensive prior works have studied how long attackers remain active within personal accounts, but none have studied this characteristic in compromised enterprise accounts. Thomas et al. [35] studied account hijacking in the context of social media by analyzing over 40 million tweets a day over a ten-month period originating from personal accounts on Twitter. They found that 60% of Twitter account compromises last a single day and 90% of compromises lasted fewer than 5 days. However, in our work with compromised enterprise accounts, we find that in 37% of accounts, attackers maintain their access for 1 or more weeks.

Onaolapo et al. [30] also found that the vast majority of accesses to their honey accounts lasted a few minutes or less. However, their work also notes that for about 10% of accesses by "gold digger" attackers (those that search for sensitive information within an account) and for most accesses by "curious" attackers (those that repeatedly log in to check for new information), attacker activity lasted several days. These two modalities, of short and long compromise durations, also manifests itself in our results, where attackers in nearly half of the compromised accounts in our dataset conducted all of their activity within one day, but over one-third of hijacked accounts experienced attacker activity across multiple days or weeks.

Attacker Account Usage Patterns. Onaolapo et al. also devised a taxonomy of attacker activity and categorized four different attacker types (curious, gold diggers, spammers, and hijackers) based on personal honeypot accounts leaked to paste sites, underground forums, and information-stealing malware. Additionally, Onaolapo et al. found that the largest proportion of "gold digger" accesses came from honey accounts leaked on underground forums where credentials are shared among attackers. In our work, we explore the potential for an economy of compromised enterprise accounts and the different modes in which attackers access these hijacked accounts. We estimate that in 50% of our sample of enterprise accounts, a single attacker conducts both the compromise and utilization of the account. Additionally, we find that roughly one-third of accounts in our dataset appear to be accessed by multiple attackers; one explanation for this could be the existence of a specialized market for compromised enterprise accounts where one attacker conducts the compromise and another attacker likely buys access to the compromised account and obtains value from the account (e.g., by accessing sensitive information or sending spam or phishing emails). Such an economy, where compromised enterprise accounts are also sold in underground forums, would be consistent with the findings in Onaolapo et al.

Uses of Compromised Accounts. Much of the prior work in the space of enterprise and personal accounts has studied attacker activity from the perspective of detecting phishing emails. For example, Ho et al. [22] conducted the first large-scale detection of lateral phishing attacks in enterprise accounts. We find that within the space of compromised enterprise accounts, email-related applications still seem to be the most common and desired way attackers obtain information within accounts. This suggests that either many enterprise cloud accounts may not have access to interesting data outside of email or that attackers have yet to exploit these additional sources of information in enterprise accounts. As a result, email remains an important direction of analysis within the space of compromised enterprise accounts.

6   Summary

In this work, we presented a large-scale characterization of attacker activity in compromised enterprise accounts. We developed and evaluated an anomaly-based forensic technique for distinguishing between attacker activity and benign activity, enabling us to perform fine-grained analysis of real-world attacker behavior. We found that attackers dwell in enterprise accounts for long periods of time, indicating that in some situations, non-real-time detectors that leverage more computationally expensive approaches and features can still provide significant defensive value. Based on the timing of attacker behavior, we infer that a specialized market for compromised accounts might exist, with some attackers developing skills specific for stealing credentials and other attackers specializing in how to extract information and value from a hijacked account. Finally, we find that most attackers in our dataset do not access many applications outside of email, which suggests that attackers have yet to explore the wide-range of information within cloud applications.

Acknowledgements. We thank Professor Raluca Ada Popa and the anonymous reviewers for their extremely valuable feedback. This work was supported in part by the Hewlett Foundation through the Center for Long-Term Cybersecurity, an NSF GRFP Fellowship, and by generous gifts from Google and Facebook.

A   Rule Set Extended Details

A.1   Extended Details on Applying Rule Set

After applying our rule set on the original set of 989 compromised users, we obtained 653 compromised users that had at least one attacker event classified. Across these 653 compromised users, our attacker rule set labeled 17,842 audit events as attacker-related. Figure 6 shows the distribution of compromised accounts among organizations. 98 of the 111 organizations (89%) had 1–5 compromised users, 12 organizations had 6–200 compromised users, and 1 organization had over 200 compromised users, precisely 206. Moreover, 68% of the 653 compromised accounts belong to 6 organizations. As a result, it is possible that one or a few attackers specifically targeted those 6 organizations. Therefore, to ensure that we obtain many different attackers and our results are not biased by a few attackers that compromise many accounts, we grouped each of the 653 compromised users by organization and month of earliest attack event flagged by our rule set and randomly selected one compromised user from each group. This resulted in a final sample of 159 compromised users across the 111 organizations.

Fig. 6. Categorization of the 111 organizations in our dataset based on number of compromised user accounts.

B   Modes of Attackers: Extended Analysis

B.1   Stability of IP Addresses

One can argue that the low geolocation Jaccard similarity coefficients might be a result of attackers using unstable anonymized IP proxies or even Tor.

For each of the 74 accounts that had max attacker interarrival times of more than 1 day, we computed the number of unique hours and number of unique country subdivisions seen across all attack events after the account's respective max attacker interarrival time. For each account, we calculated the following stability ratio of the form

$$\text{stability} = \frac{\text{number of unique country subdivisions}}{\text{number of unique login hours}}.$$

If attackers are using unstable proxy services or Tor, we would expect this ratio to be large for many of the enterprise accounts. As we can see from Fig. 7, which shows a CDF of the stability ratios for each of the 74 enterprise accounts, 85% of the accounts have stability ratios of at most 1 and 45% of the accounts have stability ratios less than 1. After looking into the enterprise account that had a stability ratio of 9.67, it was obvious that the attacker was using a specialized proxy service that generated a different IP address upon each login. In general, if attackers are using proxy services to obtain IP addresses, these services seem to be fairly stable and as a result, geolocation seems to be a viable way to distinguish between different attackers.

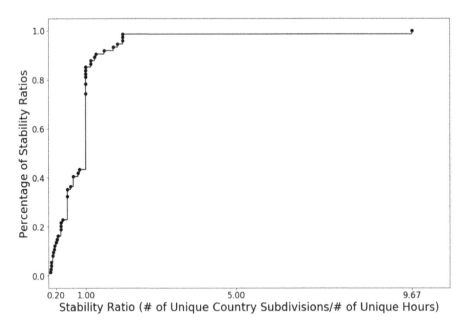

Fig. 7. CDF of the Stability Ratios for each of the 74 Compromised Enterprise Accounts

B.2   Activity Analysis of Specialized Attackers

For the 50 enterprise accounts in which we believe there are two sets of attackers (one set of attackers that performs the compromise and a second set of attackers that purchases the accounts and utilizes them), we are interested in determining if the second set of attackers inflicts more damage to the account than the first set. We developed an *application access rate* metric that measures the number of Office 365 applications accessed by attack events divided by the number of unique hours the attack events span over a certain time period. For each of the 50 accounts, we computed the *application access rate* before and after the max attacker interarrival time and in 30 of the 50 accounts (60%), we find that the *application access rate* after the max attacker interarrival time is larger than that before the max attacker interarrival time. Therefore, this analysis serves as a starting point for understanding the impact of credential selling and early mitigation of compromised enterprise accounts before they are sold to future attackers.

C   How Enterprise Accounts Are Compromised

There are many ways in which enterprise accounts are compromised [1]. Some common methods include phishing, lateral phishing [22], password reuse, and the compromise of web-based databases. In this section, we analyze how enterprise accounts are compromised from the perspective of data breaches.

Table 1. Table representing the number of organizations within each economic sector had at least one of its employee accounts found in the data breach.

Economic sector	Total
Consumer	1
Education	11
Food	1
Government	1
Health	2
Industrials	4
Technology	1
Tourism	1
Grand total	23

Data Breaches. We obtained data from a 3rd party data breach alert provider, whom we will keep anonymous for security purposes, that mines the criminal underground and dark web for compromised credentials involved in breaches of online company databases. From our dataset of 159 compromised enterprise accounts, 31 of the accounts (20%) were involved in data breaches. Users of these accounts likely used their enterprise email address to create personal accounts on websites and when the websites' databases were breached, their associated personal account credentials were leaked. As a result, if these users reused credentials across their personal and enterprise accounts, their corresponding enterprise account was also likely compromised through the same data breach.

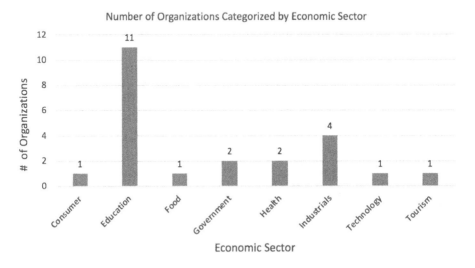

Fig. 8. Bar chart of number of organizations within each economic sector that had at least one of its employee accounts found in a data breach.

Figure 8 and Table 1 display economic sectors and the number of organizations within those economic sectors that had at least one of their accounts involved in a data breach. The 31 enterprise accounts belong to 21% of the organizations in our dataset (23 out of 111 organizations). We can see these 23 organizations span 8 of the 15 economic sectors. Although data breaches and credential leaks do not seem to discriminate against economic sectors, the education and industrials sectors seem to be hit the hardest in our dataset; there were 11 education organizations that had at least one compromised enterprise account found in a data breach and similarly, 4 industrials organizations.

From our findings, educational accounts, such as those belonging to .edu organizations, are the most common accounts involved in data breaches and credential leaks. In many cases, users of these academic accounts tend to also create personal accounts on study websites and password reuse is common; as a result, if the databases backing the websites are breached, then the original academic accounts are also subject to compromise. There has been previous research in the field of analyzing the lure of compromising academic accounts, such as the work done by Zhang et al. [25]. Zhang et al. note that academic accounts often offer free and unrestrained access to information due to less stringent security restrictions on these accounts. In addition, given that universities and schools are dormant for periods of time during the year and that upon graduation, users rarely access their educational accounts, attackers can go unnoticed for certain amounts of time in these accounts.

The findings in this section offer an insight into how enterprise accounts can be compromised. We saw that 21% of enterprise accounts were found in a data breach of online company databases; although we don't know for sure if these enterprise accounts were compromised as a result of the data breach, we nevertheless show that data breaches are fairly common among enterprise accounts and credential reuse with personal accounts can cause a lot of damage. As a result, enterprises should frequently remind their employees of the dangers of credential reuse among their accounts to avoid additional compromises of their accounts.

References

1. 10 ways companies get hacked. https://www.cnbc.com/2012/07/06/10-Ways-Companies-Get-Hacked.html. Accessed 27 Apr 2020
2. Barracuda sentinel. https://barracuda.com/products/sentinel. Accessed 29 Mar 2020
3. Detailed properties in the office 365 audit log. https://docs.microsoft.com/en-us/microsoft-365/compliance/detailed-properties-in-the-office-365-audit-log?view=o365-worldwide. Accessed 29 Mar 2020
4. Message resource type. https://docs.microsoft.com/en-us/graph/api/resources/message?view=graph-rest-1.0. Accessed 30 Mar 2020
5. Microsoft azure portal. https://azure.microsoft.com/en-us/features/azure-portal/. Accessed 30 Apr 2020
6. Office 365 management activity API schema. https://docs.microsoft.com/en-us/office/office-365-management-api/office-365-management-activity-api-schema#common-schema. Accessed 29 Mar 2020
7. Retraining models on new data. https://docs.aws.amazon.com/machine-learning/latest/dg/retraining-models-on-new-data.html. Accessed 28 Mar 2020
8. 2019 internet crime report released, February 2020. https://www.fbi.gov/news/stories/2019-internet-crime-report-released-021120
9. Abu-Nimeh, S., Nappa, D., Wang, X., Nair, S.: A comparison of machine learning techniques for phishing detection. In: Proceedings of the Anti-Phishing Working Groups 2nd Annual ECrime Researchers Summit, eCrime 2007, pp. 60–69. Association for Computing Machinery, New York (2007). https://doi.org/10.1145/1299015.1299021
10. Auth0: Protect your users with anomaly detection. https://auth0.com/learn/anomaly-detection/. Accessed 27 Mar 2020
11. Bergholz, A., Chang, J.H., Paass, G., Reichartz, F., Strobel, S.: Improved phishing detection using model-based features. In: CEAS (2008)
12. Blundo, C., De Cristofaro, E., Gasti, P.: EsPRESSo: efficient privacy-preserving evaluation of sample set similarity. In: Di Pietro, R., Herranz, J., Damiani, E., State, R. (eds.) DPM/SETOP -2012. LNCS, vol. 7731, pp. 89–103. Springer, Heidelberg (2013). https://doi.org/10.1007/978-3-642-35890-6_7

13. Bursztein, E., et al.: Handcrafted fraud and extortion: manual account hijacking in the wild. In: Proceedings of 14th ACM IMC (2014)
14. Cidon, A., Gavish, L., Bleier, I., Korshun, N., Schweighauser, M., Tsitkin, A.: High precision detection of business email compromise. In: 28th USENIX Security Symposium (USENIX Security 19), Santa Clara, CA, pp. 1291–1307. USENIX Association, August 2019. https://www.usenix.org/conference/usenixsecurity19/presentation/cidon
15. Doerfler, P., et al.: Evaluating login challenges as a defense against account takeover. In: The World Wide Web Conference, WWW 2019 (2019)
16. Egele, M., Stringhini, G., Kruegel, C., Vigna, G.: COMPA: detecting compromised accounts on social networks. In: Proceedings of 20th ISOC NDSS (2013)
17. Fairbanks, K.D., Lee, C.P., Xia, Y.H., Owen, H.L.: Timekeeper: a metadata archiving method for honeypot forensics. In: 2007 IEEE SMC Information Assurance and Security Workshop, pp. 114–118 (2007)
18. FBI: Business E-Mail Compromise The 12 Billion Dollar Scam, July 2018. https://www.ic3.gov/media/2018/180712.aspx
19. Fette, I., Sadeh, N., Tomasic, A.: Learning to detect phishing emails. In: Proceedings of the 16th International Conference on World Wide Web, WWW 2007, pp. 649–656. Association for Computing Machinery, New York (2007). https://doi.org/10.1145/1242572.1242660
20. Gascon, H., Ullrich, S., Stritter, B., Rieck, K.: Reading between the lines: content-agnostic detection of spear-phishing emails. In: Bailey, M., Holz, T., Stamatogiannakis, M., Ioannidis, S. (eds.) RAID 2018. LNCS, vol. 11050, pp. 69–91. Springer, Cham (2018). https://doi.org/10.1007/978-3-030-00470-5_4
21. Hemmati, H., Briand, L.: An industrial investigation of similarity measures for model-based test case selection. In: 2010 IEEE 21st International Symposium on Software Reliability Engineering, pp. 141–150 (2010)
22. Ho, G., et al.: Detecting and characterizing lateral phishing at scale. In: 28th {USENIX} Security Symposium ({USENIX} Security 19) (2019)
23. Ho, G., Sharma, A., Javed, M., Paxson, V., Wagner, D.: Detecting credential spearphishing attacks in enterprise settings. In: Proceedings of 26th USENIX Security (2017)
24. Hu, X., Li, B., Zhang, Y., Zhou, C., Ma, H.: Detecting compromised email accounts from the perspective of graph topology. In: Proceedings of the 11th International Conference on Future Internet Technologies, CFI 2016, pp. 76–82. Association for Computing Machinery, New York (2016). https://doi.org/10.1145/2935663.2935672
25. Zhang, J., Berthier, R., Rhee, W., Bailey, M., Pal, P., Jahanian, F., Sanders, W.H.: Safeguarding academic accounts and resources with the university credential abuse auditing system. In: IEEE/IFIP International Conference on Dependable Systems and Networks (DSN 2012), pp. 1–8 (2012)
26. Liu, B., Liu, Z., Zhang, J., Wei, T., Zou, W.: How many eyes are spying on your shared folders? In: Proceedings of the 2012 ACM Workshop on Privacy in the Electronic Society, WPES 2012, pp. 109–116 Association for Computing Machinery, New York (2012). https://doi.org/10.1145/2381966.2381982
27. Malekian, D., Hashemi, M.R.: An adaptive profile based fraud detection framework for handling concept drift. In: 2013 10th International ISC Conference on Information Security and Cryptology (ISCISC), pp. 1–6 (2013)
28. MaxMind: Maxmind database website. https://www.maxmind.com/en/home
29. Niwattanakul, S., Singthongchai, J., Naenudorn, E., Wanapu, S.: Using of Jaccard coefficient for keywords similarity, March 2013

30. Onaolapo, J., Mariconti, E., Stringhini, G.: What happens after you are pwnd: Understanding the use of leaked webmail credentials in the wild. In: Proceedings of the 2016 Internet Measurement Conference, IMC 2016, pp. 65–79. Association for Computing Machinery, New York (2016). https://doi.org/10.1145/2987443.2987475

31. Roberts, J.J.: Homeland Security Chief Cites Phishing as Top Hacking Threat, November 2016. http://fortune.com/2016/11/20/jeh-johnson-phishing/

32. Robertson, W., Vigna, G., Krügel, C., Kemmerer, R.: Using generalization and characterization techniques in the anomaly-based detection of web attacks. In: Proceedings of the NDSS, January 2006

33. Shah, N., Ho, G., Schweighauser, M., Afifi, M.H., Cidon, A., Wagner, D.: A large-scale analysis of attacker activity in compromised enterprise accounts (extended report). In arxiv (2020)

34. Stringhini, G., Thonnard, O.: That ain't you: blocking spearphishing through behavioral modelling. In: Almgren, M., Gulisano, V., Maggi, F. (eds.) DIMVA 2015. LNCS, vol. 9148, pp. 78–97. Springer, Cham (2015). https://doi.org/10.1007/978-3-319-20550-2_5

35. Thomas, K., Li, F., Grier, C., Paxson, V.: Consequences of connectivity: characterizing account hijacking on Twitter. In: Proceedings of the 2014 ACM SIGSAC Conference on Computer and Communications Security, CCS 2014, pp. 489–500. Association for Computing Machinery, New York (2014). https://doi.org/10.1145/2660267.2660282

36. Thomas, K., et al.: Data breaches, phishing, or malware? understanding the risks of stolen credentials. In: Proceedings of the 2017 ACM SIGSAC Conference on Computer and Communications Security, CCS 2017, pp. 1421–1434. Association for Computing Machinery, New York (2017). https://doi.org/10.1145/3133956.3134067

37. Thomas, K., et al.: Protecting accounts from credential stuffing with password breach alerting. In: 28th {USENIX} Security Symposium ({USENIX} Security 19) (2019)

38. Vaas, L.: How hackers broke into John Podesta, DNC Gmail accounts, October 2016. https://nakedsecurity.sophos.com/2016/10/25/how-hackers-broke-into-john-podesta-dnc-gmail-accounts/

39. Wu, C., Wang, B.: Extracting topics based on Word2Vec and improved Jaccard similarity coefficient. In: 2017 IEEE Second International Conference on Data Science in Cyberspace (DSC), pp. 389–397 (2017)

MALOnt: An Ontology for Malware Threat Intelligence

Nidhi Rastogi[1]([⊠]) [iD], Sharmishtha Dutta[1] [iD], Mohammed J. Zaki[1] [iD],
Alex Gittens[1] [iD], and Charu Aggarwal[2] [iD]

[1] Rensselaer Polytechnic Institute, Troy, NY 12180, USA
{raston2,duttas,gittea}@rpi.edu, zaki@cs.rpi.edu
[2] IBM T. J. Watson Research Center, Yorktown Heights, NY 10598, USA
charu@us.ibm.com

Abstract. Malware threat intelligence uncovers deep information about malware, threat actors, and their tactics, Indicators of Compromise, and vulnerabilities in different platforms from scattered threat sources. This collective information can guide decision making in cyber defense applications utilized by security operation centers. In this paper, we introduce an open-source malware ontology, MALOnt that allows the structured extraction of information and knowledge graph generation, especially for threat intelligence. The knowledge graph that uses MALOnt is instantiated from a corpus comprising hundreds of annotated malware threat reports. The knowledge graph enables the analysis, detection, classification, and attribution of cyber threats caused by malware. We also demonstrate the annotation process using MALOnt on exemplar threat intelligence reports. A work in progress, this research is part of a larger effort towards auto-generation of knowledge graphs for gathering malware threat intelligence from heterogeneous online resources.

Keywords: Malware · Threat intelligence · Ontology · Knowledge graphs

1 Introduction

Malware attacks impact every industry that is enabled by Internet technology—approximately 7.2 billion malware attacks were reported worldwide in 2019[1]. Such attacks cause loss, alteration, and misuse of sensitive data and compromise system integrity. Malware often have typical patterns corresponding to the type of industry they attack, groups of attackers behind similar attacks and means to pave their way into the target system, traces left behind after an attack has taken place, and so on. For preventing and detecting future attacks - both similar and disparate, the collection, integration, and analysis of malware threat intelligence is crucial.

---

[1] https://tinyurl.com/yxs8h6aw.

© Springer Nature Switzerland AG 2020
G. Wang et al. (Eds.): MLHat 2020, CCIS 1271, pp. 28–44, 2020.
https://doi.org/10.1007/978-3-030-59621-7_2

A malware ontology can support the construction of models that can detect and track attacks from their initial stages (such as identification of a vulnerability) through later stages (such as an exploit or data compromise). An ontology acts as a blueprint of a specific domain, containing key concepts (classes), their properties. Restrictions on classes are defined to limit the scope of the class, which is then inherited by the instances as well. Therefore, it can facilitate the aggregation, representation, and sharing of threat information which would otherwise be challenging to reproduce, reuse, and analyze at a large scale. Both human and software agents can use an ontology to understand the structure of information that is stored in a document, a report, a blog, a tweet, or any other structured, semi-structured, or unstructured information source [11].

Specifically, for malware threat, an ontology can provide a dictionary of attacks and related information that can help SOC analysts to dig deeper into their origination, attack goals, timeline, affiliated actors, vulnerabilities exploited for the attack, impact on industries as well as on humans. Such rich pieces of information can be aggregated following the ontology classes and data properties, which can significantly enhance current, future, and sometimes past analysis of online attacks, thereby curbing their propagation before a malware becomes hard to contain. In the absence of an ontology, security researchers and SoC analysts struggle to manage information from multiple sources and rely on adhoc mechanisms. There are existing attack and threat taxonomies that can be extended to a knowledge graph; however, they have their limitations that we cover in later sections. Linking common information between threat sources also becomes complex and therefore researchers are either compelled to look at attack instances in isolation or make do with available context.

The main contribution of this paper is MALOnt - an open-source malware ontology[2] which underpins the collection of malware threat intelligence from disparate online sources. MALOnt contains concepts ranging from malware characteristics to attack and attacker details. For example, malware details may include family details, attack vectors (software or hardware vulnerabilities) deployed by an attacker, targeted operating system, impacted industries, history of attacks, and so on. MALOnt can be populated with specific instances and thus, be expanded to generate a knowledge graph (KG). A malware knowledge graph reasoner can infer new facts through deduction or induction and relies on machine learning and deep learning models to greatly expand the range and scale of fact generation. MALOnt will be used as a baseline framework for generating the KG, which is part of our ongoing research. MALOnt is implemented to supplement malware threat information extraction by following the steps below:

1. Create MALOnt - an ontology for malware threat intelligence.
2. Create a malware knowledge graph by integrating malware-related information with the ontology.
3. Infer implicit intelligence from the knowledge graph using an OWL (Web Ontology Language) reasoner.

These steps will be described in detail in Sect. 4.

---

[2] https://github.com/aiforsec/MALOnt

2   Background Concepts

In this section, we cover key concepts that are used to create and instantiate MALOnt.

2.1   Threat Reports

The link between Trojan.Skelky and Backdoor.Winnti

From the first observed use of the tool in January 2013 to the present, the attackers have consistently used the same password. This is the case with three different variants of the tool. The regular use of the same password across multiple variants means itâ€™s likely that only one group of attackers has been using the tool until at least January 2015.

By identifying any other malware active on compromised computers at the same time as Trojan.Skelky, it is possible to learn more about the attackers. There were almost no signs of other malware active at the same time as Skelky in most of the organizations investigated. However, two compromised computers had other malware present, active, and in the same directory, at the same time as Trojan.Skelky.

Fig. 1. An excerpt of a threat report on Backdoor.Winnti malware family.

When a malware attack occurs or when a software vulnerability is identified, a detailed account of these actions is captured by researchers and security analysts in threat reports. Corrective measures are eventually taken to prevent further propagation of the malware, and more evidence is added to the earlier documented accounts. Threat reports are technical in nature and cover the information related to malware (a collective name for viruses, trojan, ransomware, spyware) such as vulnerabilities exploited, operating system and applications impacted, modus operandi, group or cybercriminal responsible, hash of the malware, first sighting of the attack, determined IP addresses of attack server, and so on. Other security analysts and researchers utilize these reports as a reliable source to study and analyze malware samples, adversary techniques, exploited zero-day vulnerabilities, and much more. Figure 1 shows a snippet from a sample threat report[3] describing Backdoor.Win32 (Win64) malware family.

2.2   Ontology

An ontology broadly describes concepts within a domain through classes and properties. These properties include property between defined classes and their attributes. An ontology is usually designed around a few main classes that cover the domain whose scope has been predefined. These classes may have sub-classes (more specific), super-classes (more general). The relationship between classes determines the type of interaction between them. Instances are individual instantiated examples of a class, which means each instance can have different values for data properties and be connected to other instances via object properties.

---

[3] https://tinyurl.com/y9e7m5w7.

Three classes - Malware, Location, and AttackerGroup, largely describe a malware's behavior. This can be vetted with the attack or vulnerability details captured in a few relevant threat reports. The Malware class has two sub-classes - TrojanHorse and Dropper. A property hasTargetLocation exists where the domain is determined by the Malware class and range by the Location class. Two properties exist *from* AttackerGroup class *to* TrojanHorse and Dropper classes titled usesTrojan and usesDropper respectively. A property of the Dropper class is titled deliveredIn that represents the mechanism of how the dropper is delivered to the target system.

To build an ontology, three main approaches are recommended while also engaging human expertise to build them:

1. *Top-down* - Classes are defined from the root of the class hierarchy by identifying the most general classes first [5,11,18]. This approach is preferred when the goal of the ontology is to represent distinctive features of a domain [18].
2. *Bottom-up* - One starts with the leaves in the class hierarchy and builds higher levels of abstraction along the way [5,11,18]. Relevant data sources can be used to identify concepts that are expressed in the dataset.
3. *Middle-out* - The most important classes are determined first followed by the rest of the class hierarchy. It is a combination of top-down and bottom-up approaches [5,11].

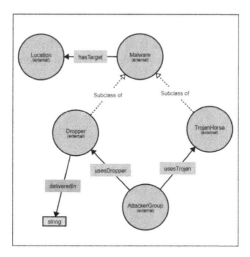

Fig. 2. Visual portrayal of a few top Classes in MALOnt using VOWL plugin in Protege.

Refer to Fig. 2 for description on a few of the concepts from MALOnt.

2.3 Knowledge Graphs

A knowledge graph is a machine-readable data repository containing a large amount of structured and unstructured data. This data is stored as triples *<Subject, Predicate, Object>*, where the predicate indicates the relationship between a subject and an object. Each entity or node in a knowledge graph has a unique identifier and may be connected via properties. A unique identifier allows capturing provenance information comprising references to threat sources of the triples. The graph structure can be exploited for efficient information extraction. Ontologies play a crucial role in building knowledge graphs (KGs). One way to build a KG is by adding individual instances to the ontology classes, and properties [11].

In addition to this, class and property instances outside of those defined by the ontology can be added to an existing KG, which allows for flexibility in KG generation. Consider the ontology explained in Subsect. 2.2. When a small portion of the ontology is populated with instances collected from threat reports, we get a small malware knowledge graph. Such as, the report titled Oops, they did it again: APT Targets Russia and Belarus with ZeroT and PlugX[4]" contains information about an attacker group, which can be mapped to AttackerGroup class. The attacker uses trojans - *PlugX* and *NetTraveler*, to target infrastructures in Europe, Russia, Mongolia, Belarus, among others. This attacker group uses a dropper *Microsoft Compiled HTML Help (.chm)* which is delivered via spear-phishing involving bespoke emails. This information is mapped to MAL-Ont classes (described in Subsect. 2.2), to generate a small part of the malware knowledge graph, as visualized in Fig. 3. A KG is not just an instantiated data of an ontology. It is a web of properties between individual nodes (also called entities) and uses a reasoner to draw connections between entities that would otherwise not be understood.

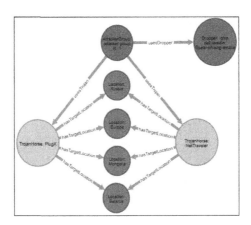

Fig. 3. Snippet of an exemplar malware knowledge graph using neo4j.

---

[4] https://tinyurl.com/yavqfb2y.

Threat Reports are annotated (see Fig. 4) using annotation tools such as Brat Rapid Annotation Tool [19], and INCEpTION to create instances of classes defined in MALOnt. Here, the text segments "PowerPoint file" and "installs malicious code" are labeled as MALOnt classes titled Software and Vulnerability respectively. The arrow from Software to Vulnerability denotes the semantic relationship between these two classes hasVulnerability.

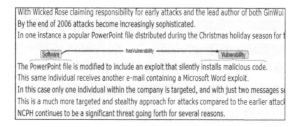

Fig. 4. Annotation using Brat [19].

3   Literature Review

We corroborate the timeliness and necessity of MALOnt in this section by explaining the gaps in existing approaches and by comparing it with the state-of-the-art standards, taxonomies, and ontologies.

3.1   Existing Malware Ontologies

Swimmer [21] presented one of the first classifications of malware and their behavior using two classes: *Malware* and *MalwareCharacteristic*. Stucco [6] expressed functionalities for capturing information on an attack although it lacked the means to store properties such as malware type (dropper, trojan, etc.) or attacker's location. Unified Cyber Ontology (UCO) [22] is based on STIX [2] and other cybersecurity standards and is mapped to vocabularies and sharing standards in the cybersecurity domain, as well as external sources such as DBPedia. To the best of our knowledge, the entire UCO is not publicly available and is broader in scope when compared to MALOnt. As normally practiced, some of the cybersecurity concepts for basic classes (e.g. MalwareCharacteristic [21]) were imported, however, MALOnt goes beyond describing just the malware attack behavior. It also captures the impacted industries, malware propagation mechanism, timeline, targeted system, prevention, and so on.

One might argue against the need for a malware ontology since there exist quite a few standards and taxonomies, as well as ontologies in the cybersecurity domain that can be used to share malware threat intelligence in a structured way. We compare some of the most prominent ones with MALOnt here. MITRE's Common Vulnerabilities and Exposures (CVE)[5] dictionary identifies publicly known security vulnerabilities in software packages. Common Attack Patterns Enumerations and Characteristics (CAPEC)[6] provides an enumeration of repeated techniques in cyber attacks. MITRE's Adversarial Tactics, Techniques, and Common Knowledge (ATT&CK)[7] provides a list of publicly known adversaries, their techniques, and post-compromise tactics to achieve their objectives. OpenIOC[8] is a standard format for sharing IOCs. CVE [9], CAPEC [1], ATT&CK, and IoCs provide static information of already discovered malware artifacts about malware attacks (among other information), which facilitates the representation and integration of collected information. STIX [2], a knowledge representation standard, is expressed in XML which does not support reasoning or identifying properties between class instances.

The aforementioned standards cannot parse multitudes of threat advisory information and present it in a meaningful, human-readable, actionable format that can be used by AI models [17] for prediction or analysis. It is our observation that the earlier work focuses on ontologies from specific threat vectors, such as malware. MALOnt differs from these largely because the domain is beyond threat Due to big data available in the cyber threat landscape, we strive to create information extraction techniques that can perform automated analysis, enable reasoning, enhance inference capabilities with minimal human intervention. This feature is currently lacking in available standards. Therefore, we propose the use of Web Ontology Language or OWL[9] as the language for malware threat knowledge representation and analysis.

3.2   Knowledge Graphs for Malware

Generating knowledge graphs for malware threat intelligence is an emerging research area. This is partly due to a limited background in KG and in adopting its concepts for security research. The paper closest to MALOnt and the proposed malware KG is [14,15], where a pipeline to create knowledge graphs from after action reports (similar to threat reports) is proposed. Existing standards and vocabularies in cybersecurity were used in conjunction with the threat reports to prepare the training dataset for the cybersecurity KG.

In contrast, a combination of vector spaces and a knowledge graph was proposed in [10]. Vector embedding can be more efficient in searching similar nodes whereas knowledge graphs enable reasoning. These complementary strengths were used to build a pipeline comprising knowledge extraction, representation, and querying of data objects which performed better than its components.

---

[5] https://cve.mitre.org/.

[6] https://capec.mitre.org/.

[7] https://attack.mitre.org/.

[8] https://www.fireeye.com/blog/threat-research/2013/10/openioc-basics.html.

[9] https://www.w3.org/OWL/.

Aside from these, multitude domain-specific knowledge graphs have been built around an existing ontology or a generic knowledge base such as Wiki-Data [7,20,23], and made openly accessible to the scientific community. While undoubtedly useful, they cater to generic concepts in the real world such as Person, Organization, Location. To the best of our knowledge, there exists no open-source knowledge graph in the malware threat intelligence domain that captures sufficient details to enable large scale automated malware threat analysis.

4 Ontology Design and Implementation

In this section, we describe the methodology and scope for defining MALOnt classes and properties, the requirement criteria, MALOnt's intended application, as well as example classes and properties.

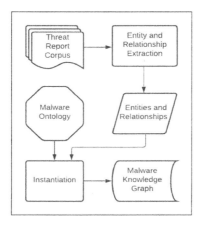

Fig. 5. Using a malware ontology to construct a malware knowledge graph

4.1 Purpose and Intended Use of MALOnt

Malware threat reports are written in natural language and describe malware attacks in detail. Information retrieval from such data feeds can be unstructured in nature, which poses several challenges for information extraction.

An ontology can serve the purpose of mapping disparate data from multiple sources into a shared structure using a common vocabulary that would further facilitate the collection, aggregation, and analysis of that data [13]. Therefore, we propose MALOnt - a malware ontology to encapsulate the concepts necessary to represent information regarding malware. The intended purpose of MALOnt is threefold:

1. To capture semantic information from threat reports by assigning individual entities or instances to a pre-defined class in MALOnt and identifying properties where applicable.

2. To use factual evidence present in the reports and infer new connections and properties between instances.
3. To serve as a foundation for creating a malware KG by populating MALOnt with individual instances from threat reports.

The steps required to achieve these goals are shown in a graphical format in Fig. 5. Once instantiated, MALOnt can extract information such as the indicators of compromise, adversary information, software vulnerabilities, attack tactics, and much more. It would also assist researchers and security analysts who gather malware intelligence from unstructured sources. Furthermore, software agents can utilize MALOnt to generate malware KGs.

4.2 Competency Questions for MALOnt

Before creating an ontology, it's requirements [11] should be gathered, defined, and scoped by answering relevant competency questions. Having these competency questions act as the north star when identifying pertinent classes and properties for proper coverage of the domain. SPARQL queries can either be used to answer a question or a narrower version of a broad competency question by running them on the instantiated ontology.

For MALOnt, the domain of the ontology is cybersecurity. In order to create the scope within the larger cybersecurity domain, over two dozen threat reports and existing ontology related sources (owl files, and research papers) were reviewed. Key terms from the reports were identified and the hierarchy of existing ontologies was studied. This helped us vet out other ontologies, import relevant classes to MALOnt, and create the class hierarchy that adequately covers different aspects of malware threat intelligence. Below are the three competency questions that broadly cover the scope of malware threat intelligence:

1. Which malware characteristics adequately define malware threat landscape? (including methods, vulnerabilities, targets, and cybercriminals).
2. What are the similar features for grouping adversaries, malware to help understand their behavior and predict the future course of action?
3. What is the impact of a given malware on an organization or industry? (financial, human life, intellectual property, reputation)

4.3 Creating MALOnt

Designing and developing an ontology is an agile process. Three stages were continuously visited and reviewed based on core-competency questions - reviewing threat reports, identifying classes, hierarchy, data properties, and evaluating existing security ontologies. The middle-out approach in creating ontology also covers the first two stages. For MALOnt, many top-level classes were created with hierarchy and data-properties abstracted from threat reports. Instances were created for these classes by capturing individuals from threat reports. In the rest of this section, we use examples to describe the middle-out approach for building MALOnt.

The pre-defined upper-level classes such as *Malware*, incorporate some of the most relevant details about a malware attack. Host, Information, MalwareCharacteristics, Malware are extracted from existing ontologies [3,6,21]. The family of a specific malware is represented by *MalwareFamily*. These two classes are joined by the property *hasFamily* where *Malware* class is its domain and *MalwareFamily* class is the range.

Thereafter, we reviewed the competency questions defined in Sect. 4.2 and identified classes such as *Attacker*, *Organizations*, and *Indicator*. Over two dozen threat reports were manually reviewed to identify key concepts that needed to be included in the ontology as new classes or properties.

For example, threat reports frequently provide valuable details about software vulnerabilities exploited by the malware, as well as specific release or version of the software product. In consequence, we included a *Software* class with two properties *hasReleaseYear* and *hasVersion*. To connect the instance for class *Software* to its vulnerability, *hasVulnerability* property is introduced.

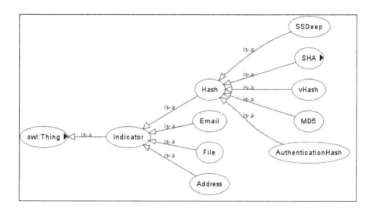

Fig. 6. Indicator class in MALOnt using OWLviz plugin in Protege [12].

4.4 Exemplar Classes and Relationships

In this section, we list out and describe some of the top-level classes and properties in MALOnt, which are essential to extract information from malware threat reports.

– Malware: The general concept of malware, which is malicious software intended to violate the integrity, availability, or confidentiality of a computer system [8]. It has four sub-classes.
– MalwareFamily: A group of malware with common properties. Often threat reports describe the behavior of a malware family (see Fig. 1) to help detect or prevent a novel malware belonging to that family.

– **Attacker:** An adversary or a cybercriminal who can cause damage to a computer system by illegal methods. It is assumed that all attackers in this class are humans.
– **AttackerGroup:** A group of cybercriminals who have homogeneous signatures of attack.
– **ExploitTarget:** An entity (a person or an organization) that is the target of a malware attack.
– **Indicator:** Distinguishable artifacts in a computer system that indicates malicious or suspicious behavior.
– **Location:** Geographic location of a place.

The Indicator class construct can be seen in Fig. 6. Since an indicator of compromise (IoC) can be of different forms (file, email, hash, address), four sub-classes are created to define them. Furthermore, a malware hash signature is of different types, and the six sub-classes of the Hash cover them.

Next, we describe a few properties that represent the semantics of the sentences and connect the instances in malware threat reports. The domain is used to define property characteristics whereas range enforces restrictions. Together they help maintain the integrity of the ontology, contain the possibility of inconsistencies, or erroneous conclusions by the automated reasoners.

– *hasVulnerability*: Bridges an exploit target or a software to its vulnerability.
  Domain: *ExploitTarget, Software*
  Range: *Vulnerability*
– *hasAttachment*: Creates link from a malicious email to the attachment it contains
  Domain: *Email*
  Range: *File*
– *indicates*: Connects an indicator of compromise to its origin. It has an inverse relation titled *indicatedBy*
  Domain: *Indicator*
  Range: *Malware*
– *usesDropper*: Connects a malware or an adversary to a frequently used measure - a dropper.
  Domain: *Attacker, Malware, Campaign*
  Range: *Dropper*
– *hasFamily*: Maps a malware to its family. There is an inverse relation of this named *hasMember*
  Domain: *Malware*
  Range: *MalwareFamily*
– *hasCharacteristics*: Maps a malware instance to its behavioral attributes
  Domain: *Malware*
  Range: *MalwareCharacteristics*

Class specific properties, called datatype properties, are shown in Fig. 2. For example, the class Software has two properties - hasVersion and hasReleaseYear.

5 Evaluation

In this section, we evaluate MALOnt by running SPARQL queries on the ontology. These SPARQL queries answer to specific use cases of the competency questions, explained in Sect. 4.2. This method of evaluation is referred to as goal modeling [4] and is considered a very effective evaluation technique to test the adaptability and consistency of an ontology [16]. If the SPARQL queries are able to extract instances as a response, it signifies that the competency questions have succeeded in covering the defined goal of the ontology.

1. **Retrieving threat information related to malware characteristics.**
   Competency question 1 can have a specific use case, where MALOnt is queried to extract attributes of different malware campaigns. MALOnt's property **targets** is selected from **Campaign** to **Organization** to get a list of all malware campaigns, their respective target organizations as well as persons (see SPARQL query in Listing 1.1).

Listing 1.1. SPARQL Query for Competency Question 1

```
SELECT DISTINCT ?instance ?p ?o
WHERE {
    ?instance a ?x .
    ?instance ?p ?o .
    ?p a owl:ObjectProperty .
    ?x a owl:Class .
    ?x rdfs:label
        "Campaign"^^xsd:string .
    ?p rdfs:label "targets"
    }
```

2. **Retrieving similar features for grouping concepts.**
   Competency question no. 2 can take various forms. Here, we show a SPARQL query that leverages the inverse properties of classes in MALOnt, to find all malware families whose member malware have left a specific IoC footprint. In Fig. 7, each instance of **Malware** class in MALOnt is mapped to an instance that belongs to class **MalwareFamily** using property titled **hasFamily**. Alternatively, there is an inverse relation of **hasFamily** called **hasMember**. Malware instances can also be mapped to **Indicator** instances using **indicatedBy** property. The inverse of this property is **indicates**.
   Once an IoC (defined by class **Indicator**) of a given malware is extracted from a threat report, the property is identified, which traces the malware back to the malware family. More insights about a malware family can be gathered through such chain properties between the three MALOnt classes.
   A SPARQL query is executed for detecting instances of *MalwareFamily* that have any member malware indicated by an *Indicator* class. The SPARQL query traverses two kinds of triple structures, ⟨*MalwareFamily, hasMember, Malware*⟩ and ⟨*Malware, indicatedBy, Indicator*⟩ in order to find the response, see Listing 1.2:

Listing 1.2. SPARQL Query for Competency Question 2

```
SELECT DISTINCT ?malware_family ?p
                    ?malware ?q ?t
WHERE {
    ?malware_family ?p ?o .

    ?malware_family a ?x.
    ?x a owl:Class.
    ?x rdfs:label "MalwareFamily"
        ^^xsd:string.
    ?p a owl:ObjectProperty.
    ?p rdfs:label "hasMember".

    ?malware ?q ?t .

    ?malware a ?z .
    ?z a owl:Class.
    ?q a owl:ObjectProperty .
    ?q rdfs:label "indicatedBy"
        ^^xsd:string .
    ?t a owl:NamedIndividual .

    ?t rdfs:label "indicator_value"
}
```

3. **Retrieving information on affected person or organization.**

   For competency question no. 3, one can extract information about affected systems, organizations, or person(s).

   The SPARQL query in Listing 1.3 retrieves a list of target objects, and accessed information from those objects by a specific attacker group. This query can retrieve all information of a particular AttackerGroup entity using properties where AttackerGroup is the domain.

Listing 1.3. SPARQL Query for Competency Question 3

```
SELECT DISTINCT ?instance ?p ?o ?q
WHERE {
        ?instance ?p ?o .
        ?instance a ?x .
        ?instance rdfs:label
            "AttackerGroup1"^^xsd:string .
        ?p a owl:ObjectProperty .
        ?x a owl:Class .
        ?p rdfs:label ?q .
        ?o a ?object .
        ?object a owl:Class .
}
```

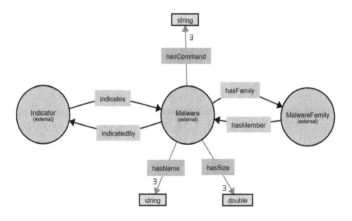

Fig. 7. Inverse properties in MALOnt using VOWL plugin in Protege.

6   Application of MALOnt

In this section, we demonstrate the process of creating a part of the KG (due to space constraints) by instantiating MALOnt with over a dozen threat reports. We also explain how the reasoner can be used to retrieve information by capturing it from multiple threat reports by executing SPARQL queries on the exemplar KG.

6.1   Annotating Threat Reports

MALOnt has been instantiated with open-source threat reports[10] that were published between the years 2006 to 2020. Many of these reports have been published by reputed organizations working within the cybersecurity domain. These reports provide a range of coverage on malware threats prominent at the time of publication. A few other reports focus on homogeneous attributes of various attacks caused by malware.

For example, a report[11] published in 2011 covers details on a set of operations known as Night Dragon. Another report[12] published in 2013, focuses on Night Dragon, Stuxnet, and Shamoon. Annotating different kinds of reports in the corpus allows deeper and wider range of details on a particular malware attack.

Threat reports were manually annotated by the authors and reviewed by a security expert. The annotated values from the threat reports were used to instantiate various concepts of MALOnt. In this step, values are assigned to instances of MALOnt classes and properties. In Fig. 8 the snippet of the malware KG depicts modeling of threat data collected from reports using classes and properties from the MALOnt ontology.

---

[10] https://tinyurl.com/y9shcvpd.
[11] https://tinyurl.com/y5veq59m.
[12] https://tinyurl.com/y52axjtf.

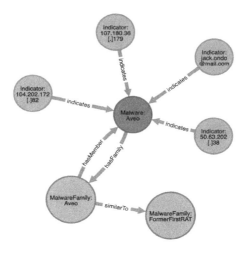

Fig. 8. Exemplar knowledge graph based on MALOnt in neo4j

7   Conclusion and Future Work

In this paper, we propose MALOnt - an ontology for malware threat intelligence by defines 68 classes, 31 properties, and 13 properties for representing malware attacks. We have used the middle-out approach for creating ontologies to review the top classes as well create classes that would be mandatory for a malware threat report. While this is work in progress, we have annotated dozens of threat reports manually to eventually feed the annotations to train predictive named entity recognition models. As future work, MALOnt will further formalize the implicit assumptions of the malware threat domain in order to build a sustainable knowledge graph. For this, annotated malware threat reports will continue to be reviewed and instantiated for MALOnt classes and relations.

Acknowledgement. This work is supported by the IBM AI Research Collaboration (AIRC). The authors would like to thank RPI researchers Shruthi Chari and Dr. Oshani Seneviratne for evaluating MALOnt and for ensuring that best practices are followed during ontology generation; Destin Lee for putting together the ontology and knowledge graph figures, and instantiating threat intelligence reports.

References

1. Barnum, S.: Common attack pattern enumeration and classification (CAPEC) schema description, vol. 3. Cigital Inc. (2008). http://capec.mitre.org/documents/documentation/CAPEC_Schema_Description_v1
2. Barnum, S.: Standardizing cyber threat intelligence information with the structured threat information expression (STIX). Mitre Corp. **11**, 1–22 (2012)
3. Costa, D.L., Albrethsen, M.J., Collins, M.L.: Insider threat indicator ontology. Technical report. Carnegie Mellon University Pittsburgh PA United States (2016)

4. Fernandes, P.C.B., Guizzardi, R.S., Guizzardi, G.: Using goal modeling to capture competency questions in ontology-based systems. J. Inf. Data Manag. **2**(3), 527–527 (2011)
5. Hendler, J., Ding, Y.: Synthesis Lectures on the Semantic Web: Theory and Technology. Morgan & Claypool, San Rafael (2012)
6. Iannacone, M., et al.: Developing an ontology for cyber security knowledge graphs. In: Proceedings of the 10th Annual Cyber and Information Security Research Conference, pp. 1–4 (2015)
7. Lockard, C., Dong, X.L., Einolghozati, A., Shiralkar, P.: CERES: distantly supervised relation extraction from the semi-structured web. Proc. VLDB Endow. **11**(10), 1084–1096 (2018)
8. Mavroeidis, V., Bromander, S.: Cyber threat intelligence model: an evaluation of taxonomies, sharing standards, and ontologies within cyber threat intelligence. In: 2017 European Intelligence and Security Informatics Conference (EISIC), pp. 91–98. IEEE (2017)
9. Mell, P., Scarfone, K., Romanosky, S.: A complete guide to the common vulnerability scoring system version 2.0. In: Published by FIRST-Forum of Incident Response and Security Teams, vol. 1, p. 23 (2007)
10. Mittal, S., Joshi, A., Finin, T.: Thinking, fast and slow: Combining vector spaces and knowledge graphs. arXiv preprint arXiv:1708.03310 (2017)
11. Noy, N.F., McGuinness, D.L., et al.: Ontology development 101: a guide to creating your first ontology (2001)
12. Noy, N.F., Sintek, M., Decker, S., Crubézy, M., Fergerson, R.W., Musen, M.A.: Creating semantic web contents with protege-2000. IEEE Intell. Syst. **16**(2), 60–71 (2001)
13. Oltramari, A., Cranor, L.F., Walls, R.J., McDaniel, P.D.: Building an ontology of cyber security. In: Semantic Technology for Intelligence, Defense and Security, pp. 54–61. Citeseer (2014)
14. Pingle, A., Piplai, A., Mittal, S., Joshi, A., Holt, J., Zak, R.: RelExt: relation extraction using deep learning approaches for cybersecurity knowledge graph improvement. In: Proceedings of the 2019 IEEE/ACM International Conference on Advances in Social Networks Analysis and Mining, pp. 879–886 (2019)
15. Piplai, A., Mittal, S., Joshi, A., Finin, T., Holt, J., Zak, R.: Creating cybersecurity knowledge graphs from malware after action reports. Technical report, November 2019
16. Raad, J., Cruz, C.: A survey on ontology evaluation methods. In: Proceedings of the International Conference on Knowledge Engineering and Ontology Development, part of the 7th International Joint Conference on Knowledge Discovery, Knowledge Engineering and Knowledge Management, Lisbonne, Portugal, November 2015. https://doi.org/10.5220/0005591001790186, https://hal.archives-ouvertes.fr/hal-01274199
17. Rastogi, N.: A network intrusion detection system (NIDS) based on information centrality to identify systemic cyber attacks in large systems. Ph.D. thesis, Rensselaer Polytechnic Institute (2018)
18. Semy, S., Hetherington-Young, K., Frey, S.: Ontology engineering: an application perspective. In: Wissensmanagement, pp. 499–504 (2005)
19. Stenetorp, P., Pyysalo, S., Topić, G., Ohta, T., Ananiadou, S., Tsujii, J.: Brat: a web-based tool for NLP-assisted text annotation. In: Proceedings of the Demonstrations at the 13th Conference of the European Chapter of the Association for Computational Linguistics, pp. 102–107. Association for Computational Linguistics (2012)

20. Subasic, P., Yin, H., Lin, X.: Building knowledge base through deep learning relation extraction and Wikidata. In: AAAI Spring Symposium: Combining Machine Learning with Knowledge Engineering (2019)
21. Swimmer, M.: Towards an ontology of malware classes, 27 January 2008
22. Syed, Z., Padia, A., Finin, T., Mathews, L., Joshi, A.: UCO: a unified cybersecurity ontology. In: Workshops at the Thirtieth AAAI Conference on Artificial Intelligence (2016)
23. Vrandečić, D., Krötzsch, M.: Wikidata: a free collaborative knowledgebase. Commun. ACM **57**(10), 78–85 (2014)

Adversarial ML for Better Security

FraudFox: Adaptable Fraud Detection in the Real World

Matthew Butler[1(✉)], Yi Fan[1], and Christos Faloutsos[1,2]

[1] Amazon.com, Inc., 410 Terry Ave N, Seattle, WA 98109, USA
{matbutle,fnyi}@amazon.com
[2] Carnegie Mellon University, 5000 Forbes Avenue, Pittsburgh, USA
faloutso@amazon.com

Abstract. The proposed method (FraudFox) provides solutions to adversarial attacks in a resource constrained environment. We focus on questions like the following:

How suspicious is 'Smith', trying to buy $500 shoes, on Monday 3am? How to merge the risk scores, from a handful of risk-assessment modules ('oracles') in an adversarial environment? More importantly, given historical data (orders, prices, and what-happened afterwards), and business goals/restrictions, which transactions, like the 'Smith' transaction above, which ones should we 'pass', versus send to human investigators? The business restrictions could be: 'at most x investigations are feasible', or 'at most $\$y$ lost due to fraud'. These are the two research problems we focus on, in this work.

One approach to address the first problem ('oracle-weighting'), is by using Extended Kalman Filters with dynamic importance weights, to automatically and continuously update our weights for each 'oracle'. For the second problem, we show how to derive an optimal decision surface, and how to compute the Pareto optimal set, to allow what-if questions. An important consideration is adaptation: Fraudsters will change their behavior, according to our past decisions; thus, we need to adapt accordingly.

The resulting system, *FraudFox*, is scalable, adaptable to changing fraudster behavior, effective, and already in **production** at Amazon. FraudFox augments a fraud prevention sub-system and has led to significant performance gains.

Keywords: Fraud detection · Kalman filters · Adversarial learning · Ensemble modeling

1 Introduction

Transactional fraud management is essential for ecommerce. The resulting 'arms race' is the first issue that the proposed *FraudFox* tackles. The second issue, is non-adversarial changes: the business rules/constraints do change over time, e.g., next month we may want to increase (or reduce) the number of investigations.

© Springer Nature Switzerland AG 2020
G. Wang et al. (Eds.): MLHat 2020, CCIS 1271, pp. 47–65, 2020.
https://doi.org/10.1007/978-3-030-59621-7_3

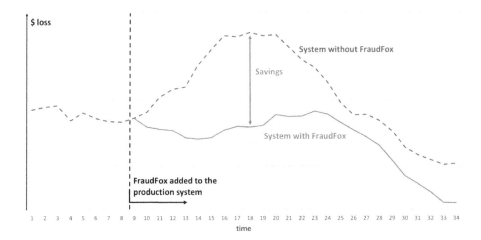

Fig. 1. Business Impact of *FraudFox*: Visible loss reduction when applying it to real word data. Losses vs. time - 1st without dynamically blending a subset of fraud indicators (blue), i.e., without *FraudFox*; 2nd with dynamically blending (orange), i.e. with *FraudFox* introduced at the dashed-black time tick. (Color figure online)

The proposed *FraudFox* handles this issue, too, by carefully pre-computing a set of 'good' solutions.

Next we address the specifications of the ADS track of the venue:

Deployed: The system is operational (see Fig. 1)

Real world challenge: Spotting fraudsters is a major problem in e-retailers. The specific challenges we focus on, are the following two: (a) how to detect fraudsters that are behaving adversarially, i.e. that are carefully trying to avoid detection. (b) how to handle changing business constraints (like number of available human investigators).

Methodology - novelty: For the first challenge, we propose an extended Kalman filter, with exponential decay (see Theorem 1 on page 8), so that it adapts to changing fraudster tactics. For the second challenge, we propose a decision surface (see Lemma 1 on page 10) and state-of-the-art optimization with PSO (particle swarm optimization), to estimate the Pareto front (see Sect. 7).

Business impact: *FraudFox* is in production, making a clear impact (see Fig. 1).

We elaborate on the main problem and its subproblems.

At the high level, we want to make pass/investigate decisions automatically, for each order like the 'Smith' order above, while adapting to both

- the (adversarially) changing behavior of fraudsters and
- the (non-adversarially) changing business constraints (e.g., 'x more investigators are available, for the next y months')

A semi-formal problem definition is as follows:

Semi-formal Problem 1

> **Given**
> - *k risk-assessing oracles*
> - *historical data (tuples of the form: [order-risk, order-price, importance-weight, fraud-flag])*
>
> **Find**
> - *the oracle-weights $\boldsymbol{w} = (w_1, \ldots, w_k)$*
>
> **To meet**
> - *the immediate business goal/constraint, and*
> - *to be prepared for unpredictable (or unplanned) business constraints in the near future.*

As we describe later, we break the problems into four sub-problems, and we describe how we solve each. Figure 1 illustrates *FraudFox* savings (green vertical arrow) post deployment (vertical black dashed line). The blue dashed line indicates fraud losses without dynamically blending a subset of fraud signals, while the orange solid line represents losses when performing this dynamic blending. Lower is better, and *FraudFox* consistently achieves visible loss reduction.

In short, our contributions are the following:

- **Automatic**: *FraudFox* adapts to new elements of ground truth, without human intervention (see Theorem 1)
- **Principled**: we derive from first principles an optimal decision surface (see Lemma 1)
- **Scalable**: *FraudFox* is linear in the input size, and quadratic on the (small) number of oracles. It takes minutes to train on a stock machine, and fractions of a second to make decisions
- **Effective/Deployed**: Already in production, *FraudFox* has visible benefits (see Fig. 1)

The paper is organized in the usual way: survey, proposed solutions, experiments, and conclusions.

2 Literature Survey

Kalman Filters. To the best of our knowledge, there are few examples of Kalman Filters used in adversarial modeling. Notable work includes Park et al. [24] whom consider a control theory setting that involved a separated observer of a system and its controller. In this setting the adversary has the ability to non-randomly erase information transmitted by the observer to the controller. Their approach to counteracting the negative impacts of the adversary is based on non-uniform sampling of the observed system. This is not unlike our approach, where we non-uniformly weight the observation data based on a noisy signal from the adversary. Another example comes from Chang et al. [8] where an ensemble method is proposed. The adversarial nature of the system is modeled using a "secure estimator" that accounts for the noise being introduced by the adversary not being zero mean i.i.d. Gaussian process noise. This secure estimator is then integrated into the canonical update equations of the KF.

Additionally, our proposal overlaps with a few other areas of machine learning which will be discussed in the rest of the section. The canonical Kalman Filter [15] is a dynamic signal processor that was initially developed in the 60's. It has long been widely applied to signal processing, autonomous driving, target tracking and so on [2]. Later, Extended Kalman Filter [13,20,23,29] and Unscented Kalman Filter [14] were proposed to solve a broader set of non-linear problems. For the Extended Kalman Filter, our work is similar to MacKay [19] and Penny et al. [26] where we make use of an approximation of the posterior from the former and also propose a method to deal with non-stationarity as in the later. However, their proposals do not consider applying the Kalman Filter to adversarial problems.

Online Learning. The other key component of our proposal is online learning. Different online learning techniques have been proposed for linear [9,34] and non-linear [12,17] models, which are primarily designed to accelerate computation time and resolve scalability limitations. In the presence of adversarial attacks, online learning becomes more powerful due to its advantages in incorporating emerging data patterns in a more efficient and effective fashion, such as [27] and the adversarial classification method from [10] (referred to as AC-method in Table 1). However, no universal solution to these types of problems has been established due to the nature of adversaries.

Ensemble of Classifiers. Ensemble learning is a popular technique used to overcome individual shortcomings of one model or another. Most popular uses of ensembles come from boosting [11] and bootstrap-aggregation [4] methods, as well as in a host of application studies [16]. Research in ensemble learning is still evolving, with some recent work focused on information extraction [18,32] or interpretability [30] of these ensembles. While other work focuses on classification improvement [22] and optimal policies for combining classifiers [6]. This includes specific applications, such as protein function prediction [33], profit estimation [1,31] and time-series forecasting [7,28]. Examples, of the use of Kalman Filters for ensemble learning include [25] and [3], however neither application concerns adversarial or non-stationary environments. An example of ensemble learning in non-stationary environments includes [21] where a simple weighted-majority vote is used to combine signals. However, the weights themselves are not learned in a principled way but are simply arbitrary weighted averages of the individual classifier performance over some time.

However, none of the above methods provides a full solution to Problem 1 in the introduction. The qualitative comparison is in Table 1

Table 1. *FraudFox* **matches all specs**, while competitors miss one or more of the features.

Property	L^{++} [21]	AC [10]	DLM [26]	*FraudFox*
Auto-adapts to adversaries		✓		✓
Auto-adapts to non-stationary	✓		✓	✓
Auto-adapts to business rec's				✓
Effective/Deployed				✓
Uses ensemble	✓		✓	✓

3 Overview of Proposed Solution

We propose to break our high-level problems, into the following four sub-problems. The first two are for the adaptation to fraudsters (with adversarial behavior); the last two are for the adaptation to changing of business constraints.

1. P1 - Fraud Adaptation: find how to automatically update the weights of the k classifiers, given new ground truth (see Problem 1 page 5). Notice that we can give importance weights to each labeled order, according to its recency, or other criteria (see page 7)
2. P2 - Anti-Gaming: given the non-stationary and adversarial environment, determine the importance weights for new ground truth orders (see Problem 1 page 5)
3. P3 - Decision Surface: find an optimal decision surface for passing or investigating orders, given the various costs and benefits of making a decision (see page 9)
4. P4 - Business Adaptation: Given the business constraints and need for quick adaption to constraint changes, find the best set (i.e., Pareto optimal) of classifier weights from Problem 1. See Problem 4, page 11.

Next, we show how to solve the four sub-problems.

4 Proposed *FraudFox*-F, for Fraud Adaptation

Here we focus on the sub-problem Fraud Adaptation. Table 2 lists the symbols and their definitions. The exact definition is as follows

Problem 1 (Fraud Adaptation)

> *Given: a new order* **with** *class label*
> *Update: the weight of each classifier* $(w_1, ... w_k)$
> *to optimize: classification accuracy*

Table 2. Symbols and definitions

Symbols	Definitions
k	Count of Oracles
$\boldsymbol{w}_t$	Weights of the Oracles (k × 1 vector) at time t
$\boldsymbol{\Sigma}_t$	Covariance matrix of the Oracles (k × k matrix)
$\mathbf{K}_t$	Kalman Gain
$\mathbf{H}_t$	Observation matrix (Eq. 6)
β	Hyper-parameter of weighting policy (Eq. 4)
α	Hyper-parameter of weighting policy (Eq. 4)
D_i	Order i's distance to decision surface (Eq. 4)
z	Binary class label
y	Model output
s_t^2	Variance of the activation function

Our approach is based on taking a Bayesian perspective of canonical Logistic Regression of the form:

$$Y_t = P(\hat{Z}_t = 1|\mathbf{w}) = g(\mathbf{w}^T\mathbf{x}_t), \quad \text{where } g(a_t) = \frac{exp(a_t)}{1 + exp(a_t)} \tag{1}$$

where the predicted class label Z_t is generated using the relationship defined in Eq. 1 and $g(a_t)$ is the logistic function and a_t is the activation at time t. The activation being the linear combination of the model inputs ($\mathbf{x}$) and the weights ($\mathbf{w}$) of the model.

With the above setting, and with a new element of ground truth coming in (an order with vector $\mathbf{x}_t$, and fraud/honest flag y_t), the update equations for the weights of the 'oracles' $\hat{\mathbf{w}} = [w_1, ..., w_k]$ are given by the Extended Kalman Filter (EKF) equations:

Lemma 1 (EKF update)

$$\boldsymbol{\Sigma_t} = \boldsymbol{\Sigma}_{t-1} - \frac{y_t(1 - y_t)}{1 + y_t(1 - y_t)s_t^2}(\boldsymbol{\Sigma}_{t-1}\boldsymbol{x}_{t-1})(\boldsymbol{\Sigma}_{t-1}\boldsymbol{x}_{t-1})^T \tag{2}$$

$$\hat{w}_t = \boldsymbol{w}_{t-1} + \frac{\boldsymbol{\Sigma_t}}{1 + y_t(1 - y_t)s_t^2}\boldsymbol{x}_t(z_t - y_t) \tag{3}$$

Proof. Special case of the upcoming Theorem 1, see Lemma 2. ∎

5   Proposed *FraudFox*-I for Anti-Gaming

Here we focus on the sub-problem of updating a classifier in a non-stationary and adversarial environment. The EKF facilities the incremental learning component, however equally important, is how much influence is awarded to new observations. The fraud environment is highly non-stationary and providing more weight to new observations is similar to gradually forgetting older ones. When receiving new fraud orders we know that all observations are not equally useful. Some of the orders are not actually fraud or the fraud pattern has already subsided. Given the large volume of new observations each day, it is impossible to manually make these decisions.

Formally, the problem we propose and solve, is the following:

Problem 2 (Anti-Gaming)

> **Given:**
> – *Several labeled orders (d-dim vectors) generated from a non-stationary and adversarial environment,*
> – *and the decision surface (from problem 3, see Sect. 7)*
> **Find:** *an appropriate weight for each order*
> **To:** *maximize classification accuracy on the recent time-period*

In this section we propose two approaches to assign importance weights. Firstly, we propose a novel weighting schema which considers fraudsters attempting to game the system (adversarial). Secondly, we derive novel update equations for the Kalman Filter that accommodate non-stationary observations.

5.1 Adversarial Adaptation

Building on the idea of an adversarial domain, it is observed that those looking to commit fraud will "poke" around a system looking for holes. In doing so, a typical fraud pattern can emerge that exists close to a *decision surface* of the fraud system. Figure 2 illustrates the motivation behind our Eq. 4: Fraudsters will tend to 'fly below the horizon', flocking below our decision surface. Our proposed approach will block them. A decision surface is essentially a rule which determines when an order is passed or investigated. We assume that the weight is a function of the distance from the decision surface, where observations closer to the decision surface receive more weight. An optimal weight is difficult to know a priori. Thus, we model this weight-to-distance relationship based on an exponential distribution. The weight (γ) of observation i is given as:

$$\gamma_i = \beta e^{-\alpha D_i} \tag{4}$$

where α and β act as hyper-parameters of the model. A very practical aspect of the EKF is that it is parameter-less. However, this can lead to a lack of flexibility and so the weighting policy provides some opportunities to adapt the model. In a following Sect. (6), we describe the creation of a decision surface from a cost-benefit analysis perspective, where standard approaches to calculate the distance a point, i, to a curve can be used for D_i.

The values of (α & β) are arbitrary, however, since training is very efficient we don't need to choose them a priori but can perform a simple grid search to generate a set of possible updates to the model.

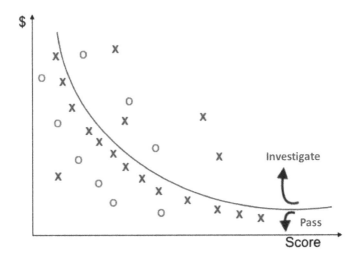

Fig. 2. Illustration of Decision Surface and Adversarial Behavior. In the (fraud-score vs. order value) plot, when we fix the decision surface (blue curve), fraudulent orders (red crosses) will probably flock just below it. *FraudFox*-I is blocking exactly this behavior. (Color figure online)

5.2   Non-stationary Adaptation

In a non-stationary environment there is cause to gradually forget previously learned patterns. With online learning, this is achieved with a forgetting function that diminishes model parameters overtime. With respect to *FraudFox*, the "idea" of forgetting can be interpreted as an increase in the covariance matrix Σ, as a larger covariance entails more uncertainty in the model and thus less reliance of the past observations. When there is more uncertainty in the prior, the model updates will place more weight on the latest observations. An EKF model can be extended to non-stationary environments by simply including a term q_t in the update equations, where $q_t \mathbf{I}$ is isotropic covariance matrix describing the impact of the state noise on the current estimate of variance in the various priors. However, we see two problems with this approach: (1) It is difficult to accurately estimate the state-noise and (2) summarize it in q_t.

Rather than estimating the state noise, we approach the problem by estimating a weight (a function of time since the order was placed) to be applied to the current observation and thus the Kalman gain update. The full derivation of the equations below is included in the supplementary material. Formally, we consider a weight a to be applied to the current Kalman Gain for purpose of a model update. Applying this weight requires the following:

Theorem 1 (EKF with forgetting).   *With forgetting parameter of a, the update equations are:*

$$w_t^* = w_{t-1} + a K_t (z_t - y_t) \tag{5}$$

$$\Sigma_t = \Sigma_{t-1} + a(a-2) K_t H_t \Sigma_{t-1} \tag{6}$$

where $\boldsymbol{w}_t^* = \boldsymbol{\mu}_t^*$ *(see Eq. 19 in proof A page 17) and* $\boldsymbol{H}_t$ *is the derivative of the logit function. In our application* $\boldsymbol{H}_t$ *is a scalar, where:*

$$H_t = y_t(1 - y_t) \tag{7}$$

Proof 1. *See Appendix A*   ■

The value of a can be chosen dynamically, and when a is chosen to be > 2 the covariance matrix increases in value with the update and thus forgets previous observations and relies more heavily on the current data point.

Lemma 2. *For* $a = 1$, *i.e., no forgetting, Eq. (5–6) become Eq. (2-3)*

Proof 2. *Recovering Eqs. 5–6 is achieved from straightforward substitution and reducing the update equations to their compact from, taking advantage of the scalar output.*   ■

In support of our argument that the added weight to new observations increases the uncertainty in the covariance matrix we provide the following proof. Where we show that the new update in Eq. 6 guarantees that the resulting Σ_t is always larger then or equal to the update from Eq. 3.

Lemma 3. *For a given new observation* x_t *with label* z_t, *we have:*

$$\Sigma_t = \Sigma_{t-1} + a(a - 2)K_t H_t \Sigma_{t-1} \geq \Sigma_{t-1} - K_t H_t \Sigma_{t-1} \tag{8}$$

Proof 3. *See Appendix B*   ■

6   Proposed *FraudFox*-D for Decision Surface

In this section we derive the optimal decision surface for taking actions on orders, a necessity for our adversarial importance weighting. For the purpose of this discussion, we simplify the actual system, and we assume that we need to choose between only two options, namely to pass, or to investigate. Then, the problem is informally defined as follows:

- given several orders, and their (price, score) for each,
- decide which ones are best to pass (vs. investigate)

Formally, we have

Problem 3. (Decision Surface)

Given:
  - *the (dollar) cost of a 'false alarm', false dismissal, and investigation cost*
  - *and a specific order with suspiciousness score* s *and value (i.e., selling price)* v

Find *the best decision we should do (accept vs. investigate), and expected value of this order, under our best decision.*

In effect, we have to combine the price v and the score s (= probability of being fraudulent), into a function $F(s, u)$ to make our decision - if $F()$ is below a threshold θ, we should accept the transaction as "honest"; otherwise we should investigate:

$$\text{decision} = \begin{cases} \text{'accept' if } F(s, u) \leq \theta \\ \text{'investigate' otherwise} \end{cases} \tag{9}$$

How should we choose the blending function $F()$, and the threshold θ? The straightforward (but wrong) answer, is to estimate the expected value: $F() = v * s$: if the price v is low, and the probability of fraud s is also low, then pass. However, this is wrong: An expensive item will almost always get investigated, potentially delaying a high-dollar order from a legitimate customer.

The solution we propose is to derive the result with a cost-benefit analysis, from *first principles*. Thus, we propose to also take into account

- c: the \$ cost of the human investigation
- m: the profit margin (say, $m = 0.1$, for 10% profit margin)
- f: the cost of friction (\$ amount reduction in life-time value or a coupon for a falsely investigated customer)
- d: the loss, from a false dismissal (usually $d = 1 - m$ but can also be impacted by external events, i.e. credit card declined by bank)

Figure 3 illustrates our setting

Reality / guess	Honest (1-s)	Fraud (s)
Honest	$v * m$	$-v * d$
Fraud	$-c - f$	$-c$

Fig. 3. Cost Benefit Analysis. Profit, for each of the four cases.

Let $s_{H,max}$ be the maximum fraud-score we should tolerate, and still 'pass' this order. Then, we can show that the resulting decision surface is a hyperbola (See illustration in Fig. 2). Next, we prove this Lemma:

Lemma 1 (Hyperbolic decision surface). *The decision surface is a hyperbola. Specifically, with the parameters as described above, the order (price v, prob. fraud s) should be passed (i.e., treated as 'honest'):*

$$\text{pass if } s < s_{H,max}$$

where

$$s_{H,max} = 1 - \frac{v * d - c}{v * (m + d) + f} \tag{10}$$

Proof. The idea is to find the expected profit for each of our decision, and pick the highest. Thus if we choose 'H' (honest), the expected profit p_h is

$$p_h = v * m * (1 - s) + s * (-v) * d$$

That is, with probability s we allow a fraudulent order, and we lose its value $(-v * d)$; and with probability $(1 - s)$ we correctly allow the order, for a profit of $v * m$. Similarly, the expected profit p_f when we decide 'fraud' is

$$p_f = -c - f * (1 - s) + s * (-c)$$

thus, we should decide to 'pass' (i.e., 'honest'), if

$$p_h > p_f$$

solving the inequality for s, we complete the proof. See Appendix C for the complete derivation. ∎

Notice that the resulting curve is a hyperbola in the (s, v) plane.

We approximate this hyperbola as piece-wise linear to simplify the implementation in the production system. Among the many ways to fit our curve we chose a multi-objective meta-heuristic algorithm based on PSO [5] due to a cheap objective function to compute and having two equally important objectives (# investigated orders and fraud \$'s captured) to satisfy.

7 Proposed *FraudFox*-B for Business Adaptation

Problem 4 (Business Adaptation)

> *Given:*
> - *the m constraints of the business (like number of available human investigators)*
> - *and the time-varying component of their thresholds*
>
> ***Find*** *an optimal set of solutions that satisfy the various thresholds of the m business constraints.*

We require a Pareto optimal set of solutions in business metric (BM) space. A solution on the Pareto frontier requires that one metric cannot be improved without the deterioration of another. Formally the Pareto set of solutions, P(Y), and a function, f, that maps a candidate *FraudFox*-F model into BM space:

$$f : \mathbb{R}^n \to \mathbb{R}^m \tag{11}$$

where X is a set of n dimensional weight vectors found with the *FraudFox*-F represented in the space $\mathbb{R}^n$, and Y is the set of vectors in $\mathbb{R}^m$, our m dimensional BM space, such that:

$$Y = \{y \in \mathbb{R}^m : y = f(x), x \in X\}. \tag{12}$$

A point y^* in $\mathbb{R}^m$ strictly dominates y', represented as $y^* \prec y'$, when y^* outperforms y' in all m dimensions. In Fig. 2 (panel B) a non-dominated solution is shown as a point that it's NE quadrant (shown in light blue) is empty. Thus, the Pareto set is represented as:

$$P(Y) = \{y^* \in Y : \{y' \in Y : y^* \prec y', y^* \neq y'\} = \emptyset\}. \tag{13}$$

In our setting, the BM space can be represented as: (1) fraud dollars captured per investigation and (2) count of investigations performed. The set of solutions is generated by using a grid search of the hyper-parameters (α and β) from Eq. 4, along with a varying ratio of positive-to-negative examples. In Fig. 4 we plot model performance results after updating using the grid search represented in BM space, where the practitioner can choose a model that satisfies the current constraints. The models on the Pareto front in Fig. 4 are indicated with a green 'X', dominated solutions are indicated with a red square.

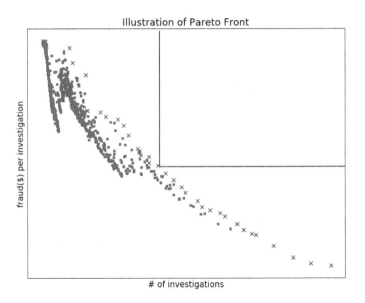

Fig. 4. Business Adaptation and Pareto Front. *FraudFox* precomputes the Pareto front, in preparation of changes in business requirements. Scatter plot of model performance in business metric space (# of investigations, vs $ fraud captured per investigation). Every point is a possible parameter choice of *FraudFox*. Points with empty light blue NE quadrants are *non-dominating* and thus form the Pareto front (green 'x' points). (Color figure online)

8   Results

FraudFox has been implemented within a larger, live fraud prevention system. In Fig. 1 (page 2) we provided a comparison (data points were smoothed via a moving average) of the missed fraud within the sub-system FraudFox was employed in, with or without it. With the introduction of *FraudFox* (dashed-black vertical line), there is a visible reduction in fraud losses.

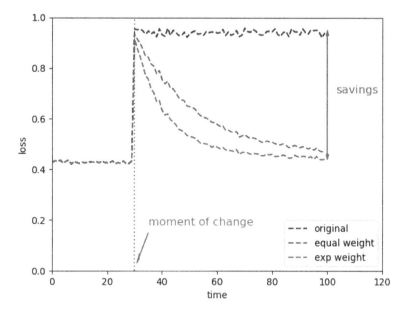

Fig. 5. *FraudFox* Adapts: Synthetic Example. As expected, both our versions (equal-weights, in 'green' and exponentially-decaying weights, in 'red') responds to a change/shock at $t = 30$, and eventually recover from the shock. Without adaptation ('blue'), the behavior suffers. (Color figure online)

Sanity-Check: Adapting to Shock. We also present a synthetic example of a one-time change, see Fig. 5. In this case, *FraudFox* adapts to the change, as expected. In more detail, Fig. 5 shows a synthetic dataset with $k = 2$ oracles, one near-perfect and the other near-random (and thus useless). At time $t=30$, there is a 'shock': the performance of the two oracles swapped. Notice that the prediction loss surged immediately as the pattern changed. We show three different strategies: (1) *no-adaptation*: baseline - we keep the original model (w), unchanged; (2) FraudFox (without exponential forgetting - Sect. 4; and (3) *FraudFox*-exp, with exponential forgetting of the older data points - Subsect. 5.2. The results in the Figure are exactly as expected: the loss jumps for all methods at the moment of the 'shock', but with *no-adaptation*, the loss stays high as expected; while both versions of *FraudFox* adapt eventually, with the exponentially-forgetting one, adapting faster.

9 Conclusions

In this work we have proposed a novel method (*FraudFox*) that solves all the sub-problems listed in the introduction (see page 1). *FraudFox* automatically adapts to a dynamic environment and provides Pareto optimal alternatives to time-varying business constraints. Finally, *FraudFox* is deployed in production and provides a solution, which is more resilient to abrupt changes in fraud behavior, while better balancing fraud losses and investigation costs.

In short, our main contributions are the following:

- **Automatic**: *FraudFox* adapts to both adversarial and non-stationary observations (See Theorem 1 and Sect. 7)
- **Principled**: we derived from first principles an optimal decision surface from investigating orders based on a cost-benefit framework (see Lemma 1)
- **Scalable**: *FraudFox* is linear on the input size for parameter updates, and takes below a second, for decisions on the order-level.
- **Effective/Deployed**: *FraudFox* is already in production, with visible benefits.

Acknowlegements. For her valuable contributions to the project we would like to thank Mina Loghavi.

A   Appendix: Proof of Exponential Forgetting Formulae

Here we give the proof of Theorem 1 on page 8. We repeat the theorem, for convenience.

Theorem 1 [EKF with forgetting]. With forgetting parameter of a, the update equations are:

$$\mathbf{w}_t^* = \mathbf{w}_{t-1} + a\mathbf{K}_t(z_t - y_t) \tag{14}$$

$$\boldsymbol{\Sigma}_t = \boldsymbol{\Sigma}_{t-1} + a(a-2)\mathbf{K}_t\mathbf{H}_t\boldsymbol{\Sigma}_{t-1} \tag{15}$$

Proof. Let's first set up some notations.

$$\boldsymbol{w}_t = \boldsymbol{w}_{t-1} + \boldsymbol{\epsilon}_t \tag{16}$$

$$z_t = h(\boldsymbol{w}_t, \boldsymbol{x}_t) + \nu_t \tag{17}$$

The underlying assumption is $E(\boldsymbol{\epsilon}_t) = \mathbf{0}$, $E(\nu_t) = \mathbf{0}$, and $E(\boldsymbol{\epsilon}_t^T \nu_t) = 0$. Furthermore, we denote $var(\boldsymbol{\epsilon}_t) = \boldsymbol{Q}_t$ and $var(\nu_t) = R_t$.

From regular EKF, we know that the update function of the mean is:

$$\boldsymbol{\mu}_t = \boldsymbol{\mu}_{t-1} + \boldsymbol{K}_t(z_t - y_t), \tag{18}$$

where $\boldsymbol{K}_t$ is called Kalman Gain with $\boldsymbol{K}_t = \boldsymbol{\Sigma}_{t-1}^* \boldsymbol{H}_t(\boldsymbol{H}_t \boldsymbol{\Sigma}_{t-1}^* \boldsymbol{H}_t^T + R_t)^{-1}$, $\boldsymbol{H}_t$ is the partial derivative of $h(\boldsymbol{w}_t, \boldsymbol{x}_t)$ w.r.t. $\boldsymbol{w}_t$, and $y_t = h(\boldsymbol{\mu}_{t-1}, \boldsymbol{x}_t)$.

Now, with the new proposed mean update function:

$$\boldsymbol{\mu}_t^* = \boldsymbol{\mu}_{t-1} + a\boldsymbol{K}_t(z_t - y_t) \tag{19}$$

we have the new error term as

$$\tilde{e}_t = w_t - \mu_t^*$$
$$= w_{t-1} + \epsilon_t - (\mu_{t-1} + aK_t(z_t - y_t))$$
$$= (w_{t-1} - \mu_{t-1}) + \epsilon_t - aK_t(h(w_t) + \nu_t - h(\mu_{t-1}))$$
$$= e_{t-1} + \epsilon_t - aK_tH_t(w_t - \mu_{t-1}) - aK_t\nu_t$$
$$= e_{t-1} + \epsilon_t - aK_tH_t(w_t - w_{t-1} + w_{t-1} - \mu_{t-1}) - aK_t\nu_t$$
$$= e_{t-1} + \epsilon_t - aK_tH_t(e_{t-1} + \epsilon_t) - aK_t\nu_t$$
$$= (I - aK_tH_t)e_{t-1} + (I - aK_tH_t)\epsilon_t - aK_t\nu_t.$$

Therefore,

$$\Sigma_t = E(\tilde{e}_t\tilde{e}_t^T)$$
$$= (I - aK_tH_t)\Sigma_{t-1}(I - aK_tH_t)^T +$$
$$(I - aK_tH_t)Q_t(I - aK_tH_t)^T + a^2K_tR_tK_t^T$$
$$= (I - aK_tH_t)\Sigma_{t-1}^*(I - aK_tH_t)^T + a^2K_tR_tK_t^T$$
$$= \Sigma_{t-1}^* - aK_tH_t\Sigma_{t-1}^* - a\Sigma_{t-1}^*H_t^TK_t^T +$$
$$a^2K_tH_t\Sigma_{t-1}^*H_t^TK_t^T + a^2K_tR_tK_t^T$$

where $\Sigma_{t-1}^* = \Sigma_{t-1} + Q_t$.

We use the same K_t as in the regular EKF and adapt that into the above equation to get:

$$\Sigma_t = (I - aK_tH_t)\Sigma_{t-1}^* - a(I - aK_tH_t)\Sigma_{t-1}^*H_t^TK_t^T + a^2K_tR_tK_t^T$$
$$= (I - aK_tH_t)\Sigma_{t-1}^* - [\Sigma_{t-1}^*H_t^T - aK_t(H_t\Sigma_{t-1}^*H_t^T + R_t)]aK_t^T$$

Note that, $K_t(H_t\Sigma_{t-1}^*H_t^T + R_t) = \Sigma_{t-1}^*H_t$. Therefore,

$$\Sigma_t = (I - aK_tH_t)\Sigma_{t-1}^* - [\Sigma_{t-1}^*H_t^T - a\Sigma_{t-1}^*H_t]aK_t^T$$
$$= \Sigma_{t-1}^* - aK_tH_t\Sigma_{t-1}^* - a\Sigma_{t-1}^*H_t^TK_t^T + a^2\Sigma_{t-1}^*H_tK_t^T$$
$$= \Sigma_{t-1}^* + a(a - 2)K_tH_t\Sigma_{t-1}^*.$$

If we let $Q \rightarrow 0$, then $\Sigma_{t-1}^* \rightarrow \Sigma_{t-1}$ and we have $\Sigma_t = \Sigma_{t-1} + a(a - 2)K_tH_t\Sigma_{t-1}$. ∎

B   Appendix: Proof of Larger Covariance Matrix

In support of our argument that the added weight to new observations increases the uncertainty in the covariance matrix we provide the following proof. Where we show that the new update in Eq. 6 guarantees that the resulting Σ_t is always larger then or equal the update from Eq. 3.

Lemma 3 [Increase in Covariance Matrix]. For $\Sigma_t = \Sigma_{t-1} + a(a - 2)$ $K_t H_t \Sigma_{t-1} \geq \Sigma_{t-1} - K_t H_t \Sigma_{t-1}$

Proof

The equality above holds when a $= 1$. Note, the right-hand side is the covariance update of the original EKF (Extended Kalman Filter). To see this,

$$\Sigma_{t-1} + a(a - 2)K_t H_t \Sigma_{t-1} - (\Sigma_{t-1} - K_t H_t \Sigma_{t-1})$$
$$= (a^2 - 2a + 1)K_t H_t \Sigma_{t-1}$$
$$= (a - 1)^2 K_t H_t \Sigma_{t-1} \tag{20}$$

Since $K_t H_t \Sigma_{t-1}$ is positive definite and symmetric, we can multiply the above by $(K_t H_t \Sigma_{t-1})^{-1}$ and the formula is reduced to $(a-1)^2 \geq 0$, where the equality holds when a $= 1$.

More rigorously, we can prove the invertibility in the following: Let M $=$ $K_t H_t \Sigma_{t-1}$. Since M is symmetric, we decompose M as QDQ^T. Here, D is a diagonal matrix of eigenvalues of M and Q is an orthogonal matrix, where rows of Q are eigenvectors of M. Hence, Eq. 20 is equal to $(a - 1)^2 QDQ^T$.

Since Q is by definition invertible, we can multiply Q^T to the left and $(Q^T)^{-1}$ to the right and reduce it further to $(a - 1)^2 D$.

Now D contains the eigenvalues from a symmetric covariance matrix and therefore all eigenvalues are ≥ 0, thus $(a - 1)^2 D > 0$ for any $a > 1$. The canonical form with $a = 1$ will always lead to min variance for a given update. ∎

C   Appendix: Proof of Optimal Decision Surface for Guessing Fraud

Here we provide the full proof of Lemma 1 on page 10. We repeat the lemma, for convenience, as well as the definitions:

- c: the \$ cost of the human investigation
- m: the profit margin (say, $m = 0.1$, for 10% profit margin)
- f: the cost of friction (\$ amount reduction in life-time value or a coupon for a falsely investigated customer)
- d: the loss, from a false dismissal (usually $d = 1 - m$ but can also be impacted by external events, i.e. credit card declined by bank)

Lemma 1 [Optimal Decision Surface]. The decision surface is a *hyperbola*. Specifically, with the parameters as described above, the order (price v, prob. fraud s) should be passed (i.e., treated as 'honest'):

$$\text{pass if } s < s_{H,max}$$

where

$$s_{H,max} = 1 - \frac{v * d - c}{v * (m + d) + f} \tag{21}$$

Proof

The idea is to find the expected profit for each of our decision, and pick the highest. Thus if we choose 'H' (honest), the expected profit p_h is

$$p_h = v * m * (1 - s) + s * (-v) * d$$

That is, with probability s we allow a fraudulent order, and we lose its value $(-v * d)$; and with probability $(1 - s)$ we correctly allow the order, for a profit of $v * m$. Similarly, the expected profit p_f when we decide 'fraud' is

$$p_f = -c - f * (1 - s) + s * (-c)$$

Thus, we should decide to 'pass' (i.e., 'honest'), if

$$p_h > p_f$$

Now we solve for the inequality, where expanding out both sides we have:

$$-[(1 - s)(c + f) + s * c] > (1 - s) * v * m - s * v * d$$

Solving for s, we have:

$$\frac{(c + f + v * m)}{(v * d + v * m + f)} > s$$

And with one final rearrangement

$$s < 1 - \frac{v * d - c}{v * (m + d) + f} = s_{H,max}$$

we arrive at Eq. 21.   ∎

References

1. An, B., Chen, H., Park, N., Subrahmanian, V.: Map: frequency-based maximization of airline profits based on an ensemble forecasting approach. In: Proceedings of the 22nd ACM SIGKDD International Conference on Knowledge Discovery and Data Mining, pp. 421–430 (2016)
2. Azuma, R., Bishop, G.: Improving static and dynamic registration in an optical see-through HMD. In: Proceedings of the 21st Annual Conference on Computer Graphics and Interactive Techniques, SIGGRAPH 1994, pp. 197–204. ACM, New York (1994)
3. Baraldi, P., Mangili, F., Zio, E.: A Kalman filter-based ensemble approach with application to turbine creep prognostics. IEEE Trans. Reliab. **61**(4), 966–977 (2012)
4. Breiman, L.: Random forests. Mach. Learn. **45**(1), 5–32 (2001)

5. Butler, M., Kazakov, D.: A learning adaptive Bollinger band system. In: IEEE Conference on Computational Intelligence for Financial Engineering & Economics (CIFEr), pp. 1–8. IEEE (2012)
6. Cerqueira, V., Pinto, F., Torgo, L., Soares, C., Moniz, N.: Constructive aggregation and its application to forecasting with dynamic ensembles. In: Berlingerio, M., Bonchi, F., Gärtner, T., Hurley, N., Ifrim, G. (eds.) ECML PKDD 2018. LNCS (LNAI), vol. 11051, pp. 620–636. Springer, Cham (2019). https://doi.org/10.1007/978-3-030-10925-7_38
7. Cerqueira, V., Torgo, L., Pinto, F., Soares, C.: Arbitrated ensemble for time series forecasting. In: Ceci, M., Hollmén, J., Todorovski, L., Vens, C., Džeroski, S. (eds.) ECML PKDD 2017. LNCS (LNAI), vol. 10535, pp. 478–494. Springer, Cham (2017). https://doi.org/10.1007/978-3-319-71246-8_29
8. Chang, Y.H., Hu, Q., Tomlin, C.J.: Secure estimation based Kalman filter for cyber-physical systems against sensor attacks. Automatica **95**, 399–412 (2018)
9. Chen, C.M., Roussopoulos, N.: Adaptive selectivity estimation using query feedback. Technical report, University of Maryland Institute for Advanced Computer Studies, College Park, MD, USA (1994)
10. Dalvi, N., Domingos, P., Mausam, Sanghai, S., Verma, D.: Adversarial classification. In: Proceedings of the Tenth ACM SIGKDD International Conference on Knowledge Discovery and Data Mining, KDD 2004, pp. 99–108. ACM, New York (2004)
11. Freund, Y., Schapire, R.E., et al.: Experiments with a new boosting algorithm. In: ICML, vol. 96, pp. 148–156. Citeseer (1996)
12. Grnarova, P., Levy, K.Y., Lucchi, A., Hofmann, T., Krause, A.: An online learning approach to generative adversarial networks. In: International Conference on Learning Representations (2018)
13. Jazwinski, A.: Stochastic processes and filtering theory. In: Dover Books on Electrical Engineering Series, Dover Publications (2007). https://books.google.com/books?id=4AqL3vE2J-sC
14. Julier, S.J., Uhlmann, J.K.: Unscented filtering and nonlinear estimation. Proc. IEEE **92**(3), 401–422 (2004)
15. Kalman, R.E.: A new approach to linear filtering and prediction problems. J. Basic Eng. **82**(1), 35–45 (1960)
16. Krawczyk, B., Minku, L.L., Gama, J., Stefanowski, J., Woźniak, M.: Ensemble learning for data stream analysis: a survey. Inf. Fusion **37**, 132–156 (2017)
17. Lakshminarayanan, B., Roy, D.M., Teh, Y.W.: Mondrian forests: efficient online random forests. In: Proceedings of the 27th International Conference on Neural Information Processing Systems, NIPS 2014, vol. 2, pp. 3140–3148. MIT Press, Cambridge (2014)
18. Lucchese, C., Nardini, F.M., Orlando, S., Perego, R., Tonellotto, N., Venturini, R.: QuickScorer: efficient traversal of large ensembles of decision trees. In: Altun, Y., et al. (eds.) ECML PKDD 2017. LNCS (LNAI), vol. 10536, pp. 383–387. Springer, Cham (2017). https://doi.org/10.1007/978-3-319-71273-4_36
19. MacKay, D.J.: The evidence framework applied to classification networks. Neural Comput. **4**(5), 720–736 (1992)
20. Meinhold, R.J., Singpurwalla, N.D.: Understanding the Kalman filter. Am. Stat. **37**(2), 123–127 (1983)
21. Muhlbaier, M.D., Polikar, R.: An ensemble approach for incremental learning in nonstationary environments. In: Haindl, M., Kittler, J., Roli, F. (eds.) MCS 2007. LNCS, vol. 4472, pp. 490–500. Springer, Heidelberg (2007). https://doi.org/10.1007/978-3-540-72523-7_49

22. Narassiguin, A., Elghazel, H., Aussem, A.: Dynamic ensemble selection with probabilistic classifier chains. In: Ceci, M., Hollmén, J., Todorovski, L., Vens, C., Džeroski, S. (eds.) ECML PKDD 2017. LNCS (LNAI), vol. 10534, pp. 169–186. Springer, Cham (2017). https://doi.org/10.1007/978-3-319-71249-9_11

23. Niranjan, M.: Sequential Bayesian computation of logistic regression models. In: Proceedings of the IEEE International Conference on Acoustics, Speech, and Signal Processing, vol. 2, pp. 1065–1068. IEEE (1999)

24. Park, S.Y., Sahai, A.: Intermittent Kalman filtering with adversarial erasures: eigenvalue cycles again. In: 52nd IEEE Conference on Decision and Control, pp. 6073–6078. IEEE (2013)

25. Peel, L.: Data driven prognostics using a Kalman filter ensemble of neural network models. In: 2008 International Conference on Prognostics and Health Management, pp. 1–6. IEEE (2008)

26. Penny, W.D., Roberts, S.J.: Dynamic logistic regression. In: International Joint Conference on Neural Networks, IJCNN 1999, vol. 3, pp. 1562–1567. IEEE (1999)

27. Quanrud, K., Khashabi, D.: Online learning with adversarial delays. In: Cortes, C., Lawrence, N.D., Lee, D.D., Sugiyama, M., Garnett, R. (eds.) Advances in Neural Information Processing Systems, vol. 28, pp. 1270–1278. Curran Associates, Inc. (2015)

28. Saadallah, A., Priebe, F., Morik, K.: A drift-based dynamic ensemble members selection using clustering for time series forecasting. In: Brefeld, U., Fromont, E., Hotho, A., Knobbe, A., Maathuis, M., Robardet, C. (eds.) ECML PKDD 2019. LNCS (LNAI), vol. 11906, pp. 678–694. Springer, Cham (2020). https://doi.org/10.1007/978-3-030-46150-8_40

29. Sorenson, H.: Kalman Filtering: Theory and Application. IEEE Press selected reprint series, IEEE Press (1985). https://books.google.com/books?id=2pgeAQAAIAAJ

30. Tolomei, G., Silvestri, F., Haines, A., Lalmas, M.: Interpretable predictions of tree-based ensembles via actionable feature tweaking. In: Proceedings of the 23rd ACM SIGKDD International Conference on Knowledge Discovery and Data Mining, pp. 465–474 (2017)

31. Xu, Q., Sharma, V.: Ensemble sales forecasting study in semiconductor industry. ICDM 2017. LNCS (LNAI), vol. 10357, pp. 31–44. Springer, Cham (2017). https://doi.org/10.1007/978-3-319-62701-4_3

32. Ye, T., Zhou, H., Zou, W.Y., Gao, B., Zhang, R.: RapidScorer: fast tree ensemble evaluation by maximizing compactness in data level parallelization. In: Proceedings of the 24th ACM SIGKDD International Conference on Knowledge Discovery & Data Mining, pp. 941–950 (2018)

33. Yu, G., Domeniconi, C., Rangwala, H., Zhang, G., Yu, Z.: Transductive multi-label ensemble classification for protein function prediction. In: Proceedings of the 18th ACM SIGKDD International Conference on Knowledge Discovery and Data Mining, pp. 1077–1085 (2012)

34. Zhang, T.: Solving large linear prediction problems using stochastic gradient descent algorithms. In: Proceedings of the Twenty-first International Conference on Machine Learning, ICML 2004, pp. 116. ACM, New York (2004)

Towards Practical Robustness Improvement for Object Detection in Safety-Critical Scenarios

Zhisheng Hu$^{(\boxtimes)}$ and Zhenyu Zhong

Baidu USA, Sunnyvale, CA 94089, USA
{zhishenghu,edwardzhong}@baidu.com

Abstract. Object detection has been widely applied to safety-critical scenarios such as autonomous driving. Recent works show that object detectors can be easily deceived by small adversarial examples. While adversarial training is one of the few effective methods to improve robustness, there is no practical adversarial training on large-scale DNNs (e.g., YOLO V3 and ResNet101) over large datasets (e.g., MS-COCO and ImageNet) due to the high cost of generating adversarial examples.

In this paper, we aim to improve the robustness of state-of-art object detectors practically. In particular, we propose a two-stage adversarial training algorithm to improve the robustness of YOLO V3 successfully. Based on the experiments on MS-COCO, we come up with a refined adversarial training and corresponding insights to efficiently make the model more robust on safety-critical scenarios. We hope this work can serve as a stepping stone to seek efficient defenses against adversarial examples in large-scale object detectors.

Keywords: Object detection · Adversarial examples · Adversarial training

1 Introduction

In the past decade, Deep neural networks (DNNs) have been applied to diverse tasks such as image classification [12,15,25], speech recognition [6,8], object detection [4,20–22]. Although DNNs can achieve excellent performances in many tasks, their accuracies might drop to nearly zero when the inputs are subjected to small adversarial perturbations [14,24]. Such catastrophic failure could lead to severe consequences especially for those safety-critical scenarios (e.g., autonomous driving [1,2], biometric authentication and online content moderation).

Along with the emerging adversarial example phenomenon, robustness is becoming a more important factor in evaluating DNNs from a security perspective. Intuitively speaking, a robust DNN is the one that can correctly predict inputs with adversarial perturbations. Formally, the robustness of a DNN

G. Wang et al. (Eds.): MLHat 2020, CCIS 1271, pp. 66–83, 2020.
https://doi.org/10.1007/978-3-030-59621-7_4

quantifies the network's resilience against adversarial inputs [24]. And there are two common-used measurements of robustness: 1. the accuracy on adversarial examples [7,14] and 2. the success rate of the adversarial examples to deceive a DNN [9,13].

And adversarial training, which trains a DNN on adversarial examples, is one of the few effective methods for obtaining robust DNNs against adversarial examples. However, there is no practical adversarial training on large-scale DNNs (e.g., YOLO V3 [21] and Inception V3 [23]) due to the high cost of generating adversarial examples. For example, the authors in [14] used 50 machines to adversarially train an Inception V3 on ImageNet. And as for object detectors, there is hardly any guidance of how to generate adv examples and how to utilize them to perform efficient and effective adversarial training. The work by Zhang et al. [26] tried to explore the possibility of improving robustness by generalizing adversarial training of classifiers from multi-task learning perspective. However, this work mainly focused on PASCAL VOC dataset and showed a low accuracy on a more practical dataset: MS-COCO. Besides, no results on the efficiency of adversarial training of object detectors have been discussed or revealed. Due to the important role of object detectors in safety-critical applications, it is necessary to improve the robustness of the detectors in practice.

In this paper, we focus on how to practically improve the robustness of real-world object detectors by leveraging adversarial training. And our contributions are summarized as follows.

- We propose a practical adversarial training to successfully train the state-of-art object detector YOLO V3 on MS-COCO dataset [16].
- We verify the robustness of the trained model can be improved in terms of both increasing accuracies against adversarial examples generated by projected gradient descent (PGD) [18] and decreasing adversarial examples' success rates.
- Based on our experiment results on MS-COCO validation set, we propose a refined adversarial training to efficiently improve the model robustness on a special autonomous driving scenario.
- We also study the robustness of our adversarially trained models against adversarial examples generated by other two attacks: C&W attack [5] and fast gradient sign method (FGSM) attack [7].

The rest of the paper is organized as follows. Sect. 2 presents the background of adversarial examples in object detection models. Sect. 3 introduces our adversarial training methodology. Sect. 4 demonstrates our evaluation and the results of our adversarial training and proposes a refined adversarial training based on our evaluation results. And Sect. 5 concludes the paper.

2   Adversarial Examples in Object Detectors

Object detection aims to predict the locations of the objects along with the classes in given images or video frames, which has been widely applied in many safety-critical scenarios such as autonomous driving. While a lot of works have explored adversarial examples against image classifiers [5,13,14,18,19] and some of them [5,13,18] have become standard practice in evaluating defenses, few work studies the adversarial examples in object detectors. Compared to image classifiers, object detectors in safety-critical scenarios are more vulnerable to adversarial examples, which can either misclassify labels of the objects or mislead object location predictions in given images. Either misclassified labels or wrong locations could lead to severe consequences, especially in safety-critical scenarios. For example, a Tesla car was involved in a fatal crash caused by the failure of its forward-looking camera failed to detect a white truck [3].

Despite some research [17] claims that adversarial examples should work on most the frames in a video stream, an advanced attack [10] shows a successful adversarial example on as few as one single frame can put in or erase one object from of an autonomous vehicle. Therefore we can borrow the adversarial attacks against image classifiers to target object detectors. In this paper, we focus on the adversarial examples that can either mislead the model to misclassify the main objects or ignore main objects in images. Figure 1 provides an example of misleading YOLO V3 to misclassify cars into trucks. In addition, the adversarial example also makes the model ignore a car on the left top area.

Fig. 1. Adversarial example against YOLO V3

In this paper, we apply perturbations multiple times to get adversarial examples. And for the ease of presentation, we will use the following notations through the paper.

- $\mathbf{x}$: the clean input.
- $\mathbf{y}_{true}$: the ground truth of the input, including the coordinates of the bounding boxes; i.e., $\mathbf{y}_{true}^{box}$, and classes the bounding boxes may contain; i.e., $\mathbf{y}_{true}^{label}$.

- $\hat{\mathbf{y}} = f_\theta(\mathbf{x})$: the predictions of the model, including the coordinates of the bounding boxes; i.e., $\hat{\mathbf{y}}^{box}$ and classes the bounding boxes may contain; i.e., $\hat{\mathbf{y}}^{label}$.
- $L(f_\theta(\mathbf{x}), \mathbf{y}_{true})$: the loss on the input x with its ground truth $\mathbf{y}_{true}$.
- δ_n: the adversarial perturbation at iteration n.
- $\mathbf{x}_n^{adv}$: the adversarial example at iteration N. In particular, $\mathbf{x}_0^{adv} = \mathbf{x}$.
- ϵ: the maximum aggregate perturbation. In this paper, we consider l_∞-norm and require $\mathbf{x}_n^{adv}$ falls into the ϵ-ball of around $\mathbf{x}$ for all n.
- $Clip_{\mathbf{x},\epsilon}(\mathbf{x}_n^{adv})$: element-wise clipping where $\mathbf{x}_n^{adv}$ is clipped into $[\mathbf{x} - \epsilon, \mathbf{x} + \epsilon]$.

3 Two-Stage Adversarial Training

The basic idea of adversarial training is to augment the training set with adversarial examples. Formally, the adversarial training tries to solve the following minmax problem:

$$\min_\theta \{ \max_{\mathbf{x}' \in [\mathbf{x}-\epsilon, \mathbf{x}+\epsilon]} L(f_\theta(\mathbf{x}'), \mathbf{y}_{true}) \}, \tag{1}$$

where θ are the model parameters.

In this paper, we use YOLO V3 as a running example to demonstrate our adversarial training. We choose YOLO V3 because it is a representative model of one-stage detectors and widely used in safety-critical scenarios thanks to its fast detection capability. We propose the following two-stage adversarial training algorithm. The algorithm contains two main parts: adversarial example generation and training. We first generate different sets of adversarial examples on MS-COCO dataset by approximately solving the inner maximization problem in (1) with PGD method. We then perform two conventional trainings by solving the outer minimization problem in (1) on the generated adversarial examples.

For adversarial example generation, we focus on generating adversarial examples that can lead to misclassification of the main objects. To achieve this type of adversarial examples, we apply PGD attack on the pre-trained YOLO V3 model. In particular, we implement N-step PGD with perturbation magnitude ϵ. At each step, we compute an example that can projected gradient decrease the negative loss function (Line 5 of Algorithm 1).

To properly train the YOLO V3 with our adversarial examples without cause overfitting, fine-tuning the output layers of the pre-trained YOLO V3 is suggested [27]. However, object detectors give prediction based on the extracted features of the objects, and wrong predictions might be made based on the features before the output layer. Therefore, we adopt a two-stage training strategy. In particular, at stage one: we restore the weights from checkpoints, freeze the convolution layers, and train the output layers with big learning rate like 10^{-3}. At stage two: we restore the weights from the first stage, then train the whole model with a small learning rate like 10^{-4} and reduce the learning rate while no improvement is observed.

It is worth to mention that the parameter N; i.e., the iteration number of generating adversarial examples, and the parameter ϵ; i.e., the maximum aggregate

---

Algorithm 1. Two-stage adversarial training for YOLO V3

1: Load pre-trained model;
2: Generating adversarial examples for a super-category of images:
3: **while** $0 \leq n \leq N$ and $\hat{\mathbf{y}}_n^{label} \cap \mathbf{y}_{true}^{label} \neq \emptyset$ **do**
4:      $\delta_n = \alpha sign(\Delta_{\mathbf{x}} L(f_\theta(\mathbf{x}_n^{adv}), \mathbf{y}_{true}))$;
5:      $\mathbf{x}_{n+1}^{adv} = Clip_{\mathbf{x},\epsilon}(\mathbf{x}_n^{adv} + \delta_n)$;
6:      $n \leftarrow n + 1$;
7: **end while**
8: Training stage **one**:
9: **repeat**
10:      Read a minibatch B of training data;
11:      Do one training step of output layers of the model on B;
12: **until** reach maximum training iteration
13: Save stage one model;
14: Training stage **two**:
15: Restore stage one model;
16: **repeat**
17:      Read a minibatch B of training data;
18:      Do one training step of the whole model on B;
19: **until** reach maximum training iteration
20: Save re-trained model;

---

perturbation are two important factors that reflect how "severe" the adversarial examples are. We observe that adversarial examples that are generated with larger N and ϵ can deceive the model with higher probability than those are generated with smaller N and ϵ. The concrete results will be shown in Sect. 4. Then we will propose an improved training algorithm based on how these parameters affect the adversarial training results.

4   Evaluation

4.1   Evaluation Setup

In this paper, we adversarially train a YOLO V3 model on adversarial examples generated from MS-COCO dataset. The backbone of the pre-trained model YOLO V3 is Darknet-53.

All experiments are done on a single computer equipped with an Intel Xeon Gold 6130 CPU and an Nvidia Tesla V100 GPU with a minibatch of 32 examples. We do not train the YOLO V3 from scratch and all models are trained according to the two-stage training strategy introduced in Sect. 3. We use Adam optimizer [11] with an initial learning rate of 10^{-3} and a learning rate decay factor of 10^{-1} when validation loss stops improving. We observe that the loss tends to converge at around 32k training iterations and the loss increases after 32k iterations. Therefore, we train our models for 32K iterations except where otherwise is indicated.

For the dataset in our evaluation, the size of the image is $416 * 416$ with each pixel value in $[0, 255]$. Due to the high generation cost, we choose not to generate an enormous amount of adversarial examples. We generate adversarial examples on subsets of train 2017 and val 2017 (123k images in total) of MS-COCO dataset and train the models with part of the examples. We use val 2017 (5k images) as clean examples and the rest part of the adversarial examples to test our models. The test set does not intersect with the training set.

4.2   Adversarial Examples Severity

In this subsection, we study how severe damage can be brought by adversarial examples generated with different iteration numbers and perturbation magnitudes. To measure the severity, we introduce a metric named **success rate**. The success rate quantifies how easily an attacker can fool an object detector. In particular, given an object detector, the success rate is the ratio of successful adversarial examples to the total number of attack trials. In this paper, a successful adversarial example is regarded as an example whose main objects will be misclassified by the object detector.

How Does Perturbation Magnitude Affect Severity? We first evaluate how easily the pre-trained YOLO V3 can be fooled by adversarial examples generated with different ϵ. Fig 2 - (a) presents the success rates of the adversarial examples generated with different ϵ (from 2 to 10 with step size 2) under a fixed maximum iteration $N = 20$. We get an interesting observation from the result: as ϵ increases, the generated adversarial examples induce severer damage to the YOLO V3. The attacker has the incentive to choose large ϵ in order to fool the object detector. However, when ϵ is too large, the generated adversarial examples are perceptually distinguishable from the original images.

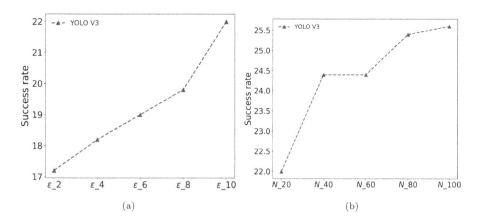

(a)   (b)

Fig. 2. (a) shows the success rates the success rates of pre-trained YOLO V3 under examples generated with different ϵ when $N = 20$; (b) shows the success rates of pre-trained YOLO V3 under examples generated with different N when $\epsilon = 10$.

How Does Iteration Number Affect Severity? We then evaluate how easily the pre-trained YOLO V3 can be fooled by adversarial examples generated with different N. Fig. 2 - (b) presents the success rates of the adversarial examples generated with different N (from 20 to 100 with step size 20) under a fixed perturbation magnitude $\epsilon = 10$. The result indicates that the attacker also has the incentive to choose large N in order to fool the object detector. However, a large iteration number requires huge time consumption. Table 1 shows that the time used (seconds) to generate 5k adversarial examples with iterations $20, 40, 60, 80$ and 100. We observe that the time consumption increases almost linearly with N while ϵ barely affects the time consumption. And we also observe that the success rate increases by around 24.5% as N increases. But when ϵ increases, the success rate increases by as much as 30.1%. Therefore, from the attacker's perspective, choosing larger ϵ might bring more benefits and choosing as large N as possible is not always a good strategy to generate severe adversarial examples.

Table 1. Time consumption of generating adversarial examples

ϵ	N				
	20	40	60	80	100
2	$10,874$	$19,738$	$30,994$	$41,932$	$50,391$
10	$10,978$	$20,814$	$31,798$	$41,862$	$50,293$

4.3 Adversarial Training Results

We perform our adversarial training using the adversarial examples generated by the multi-step PGD method introduced above. We evaluate our models on both clean and adversarial examples. Before presenting the results, let us first introduce the main evaluation metric for object detectors.

Mean Average Precision (mAP). Object detection task can be viewed as a set of independent tasks; i.e., predicting the locations for a specific category of objects. And a separate score is calculated for each category. Average precision (AP), which is defined as the mean precision at a set of recall levels, is introduced to measure the accuracy of detecting each category. To obtain a high AP, the model must have high precision at all levels of recall.

In this paper, we use mAP, which averages the AP over all categories (there are 80 categories for MS-COCO dataset), as the main metric to measure the overall performance of the pre-trained and adversarially trained models. And specifically for MS-COCO dataset, mAP is averaged over one or multiple intersection over union (IoU) values, which measure the overlap between the predicted boundary and the real object boundary. In particular, we list the mAP on all IoU thresholds (the minimum IoU value for the model to predict a positive result) used in this paper as follows.

- mAP_50: mAP at IoU $= 0.5$.
- mAP_75: mAP at IoU $= 0.75$.
- mAP_all: average mAP for 10 IoU thresholds from 0.5 to 0.95 with a step size of 0.05.
- mAP_L: mAP_all for large objects whose areas are larger than 96^2.

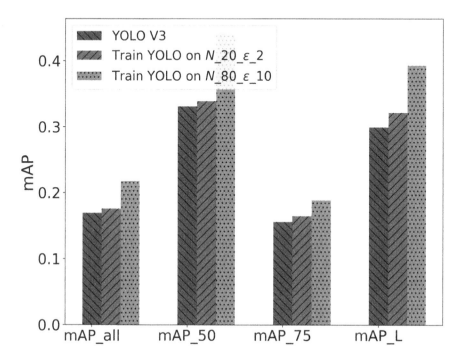

Fig. 3. Comparison pre-trained YOLO V3 and adversarially trained models under "strong" adversarial examples.

We train the model with two sets of adversarial examples: 1. adversarial examples generated by 80-step PGD with perturbation magnitude $\epsilon = 10$ (we do not choose $N = 100$ because it does not increase success rate significantly and induce high computation cost), which will be referred as "strong" examples; and 2. adversarial examples generated by 20-step PGD with perturbation magnitude $\epsilon = 2$, which will be referred as "weak" examples. We first compare the performance of models under the "strong" examples. The comparison results are shown in Fig. 3. We observe that our adversarial training with both "weak" and "strong" examples can improve the performance under "strong" adversarial examples. Especially, the improvement of detecting large objects (e.g., cars, trucks) is obvious, which might be good for the autonomous driving scenario. Later we will test the models on vehicle images to further study the model robustness in the autonomous driving scenario.

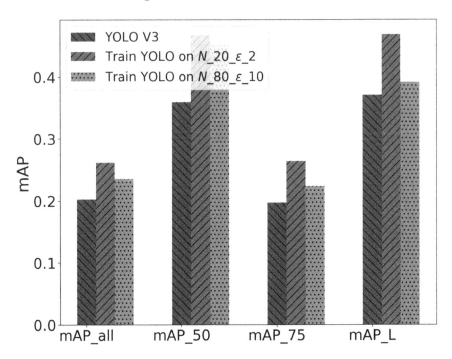

Fig. 4. Comparison of pre-trained YOLO V3 and adversarially trained models under "weak" adversarial examples.

But we also observe that the performance improvement of the model trained with "weak" examples is much smaller. Similar results can be found when comparing the performance of models under the "weak" adversarial examples (shown in Fig. 4). When testing with "weak" examples, the performance improvement of the model trained with "strong" examples is trivial. These results imply that the performance improvement of the model heavily depends on the training data. And training on a single set of adversarial examples cannot guarantee universal improvement under all adversarial examples. We also observe performance decrease on clean examples, as shown in Fig. 5. In particular, adversarial training with "strong" examples suffers significant performance drop. In both cases, the best performance is achieved when the model is trained with the same type of adversarial examples.

One possible explanation is that our adversarial training might lead to overfitting. As mentioned, we use iterative methods and do not generate adversarial examples for the whole MS-COCO dataset. Essentially, we are fine-tuning the pre-trained YOLO V3 on small datasets.

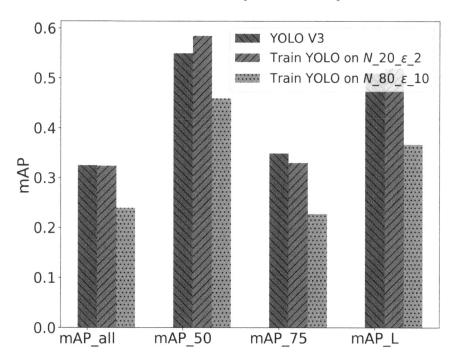

Fig. 5. Comparison of pre-trained YOLO V3 and adversarially trained models under clean examples.

4.4 Refined Adversarial Training

It is difficult to eliminate overfitting with a small training set. One naive solution is to enlarge the training set. But it is shown by a recent work that training on one-step adversarial examples does not confer robustness to iterative adversarial examples [14]. So to remain robust against the iterative adversarial examples (e.g., the "strong" examples), we cannot enlarge the training set by generating examples with very small N. In the meanwhile, the high computational cost brought by multi-step PGD prevents us from enlarging our adversarial example sets by generating an enormous amount of examples with large N. Therefore, we propose the following refined adversarial training, as described in Algorithm 2, to mitigate overfitting.

Table 2. mAP with different sizes of B'

	Ratio of $|B'|$ to $|B|$			
	0.25	0.5	0.75	1.0
mAP_all on "strong" examples	0.143	0.251	0.250	0.176
mAP_all on clean examples	0.324	0.330	0.321	0.240

Algorithm 2. Practical adversarial training for YOLO V3

...

8: Training stage **one**:
9: **repeat**
10:    Read a minibatch B of examples with small ϵ and N;
11:    Do one training step of the model on B;
12: **until** reach maximum training iteration or early stopping
13: Save stage one model;
14: Training stage **two**:
15: Restore stage one model;
16: **repeat**
17:    Read a minibatch B' of examples with large ϵ and N;
18:    Do one training step of the output layers on B';
19: **until** reach maximum training iteration or early stopping
20: Save re-trained model;

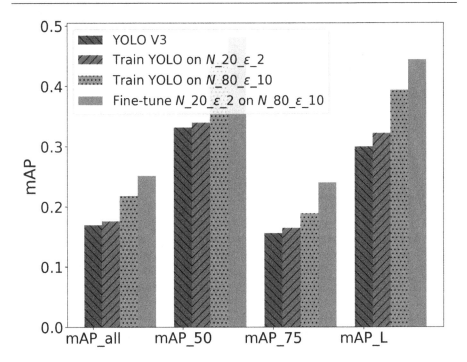

Fig. 6. Comparison of adversarially trained models and fine-tuned models under "strong" examples.

The refined adversarial training is similar to Algorithm 1 but we train the model on examples with smaller ϵ and N at stage one and then fine-tune stage one model using a small portion of examples with larger ϵ and N. And we train the whole network in stage one while we only train the output layers in stage two. Here stage two acts as a regularizer which punishes the model for being

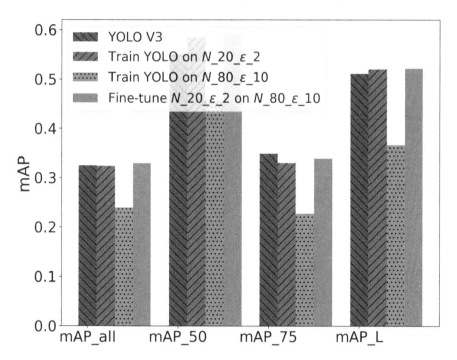

Fig. 7. Comparison of adversarially trained models and fine-tuned models under clean examples.

sensitive to the changes from B to B'. In addition, we add early stopping for both stages to further mitigate overfitting. Note that in our experiments, we find out a larger B' does not necessarily improve the robustness significantly, as shown in Table 2. Instead, a very large B' sometimes induces performance drop on clean examples.

We then compare the performance of Algorithm 2 and Algorithm 1. In particular, we use the "weak" examples ($N = 20, \epsilon = 2$) as B in stage one and use half of the "strong" examples ($N = 80, \epsilon = 10$) as B' in stage two. We first compare the performances on adversarial examples in Fig. 6. The bars filled with stripes and dots represent the mAP of the models trained by Algorithm 1 and the solid bar represents the mAP of the model trained by Algorithm 2. After fine-tuning by stage two, the model performance under "strong" examples is even better than that of the model solely trained on "strong" examples. Moreover, as indicated in Fig. 7, there is no performance drop on clean examples. Here we compare our work with that of Zhang et al. [26] in Table 3. As mentioned, there is hardly any adversarial training work on object detectors. So the comparison only validates the feasibility of our work and does not intend to show any inferior of their work. The results validate that Algorithm 2 can mitigate overfitting and improve overall performance. One possible reason is that stage one training can

Table 3. mAP comparison with previous work

	Clean examples	"strong" examples
Zhang et al. [26]	0.240	0.215
Ours	0.330	0.251

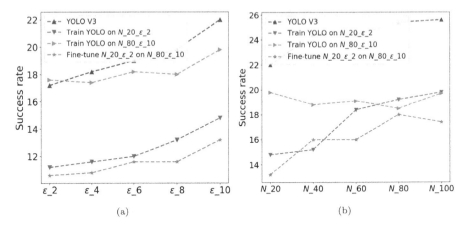

(a)   (b)

Fig. 8. (a) compares the success rates of models under examples generated with different ϵ when $N = 20$; (b) compares the success rates of models under examples generated with different N when $\epsilon = 10$.

learn the features of clean models while stage two training makes the model less sensitive to the adversarial examples with larger perturbations.

Success Rate. As introduced before, success rate can evaluate the severity of adversarial examples. In the meanwhile, we can use success rates of different adversarial examples to measure the model robustness under different circumstances. Figure 8 shows the success rates of different models under adversarial examples generated with different ϵ and N. Compare with the pre-trained YOLO V3, all of our adversarially trained models can lower the success rates. Moreover, the model (represented by the dashed line with star marker in Fig. 8) trained by Algorithm 2 is the most robust model against almost all adversarial examples. These results are consistent with the mAP measurements. From both measurements, we show that our proposed adversarial training can improve model robustness in general.

4.5   Experiments on Autonomous Driving

The overall robust improvement leads us to the following two interesting questions: can we apply the adversarial training on safety-critical scenarios? Or can we make the adversarial training even more efficient when we focus on a specific safety-critical scenario? To explore the answers, we further customize and evaluate our adversarial training on autonomous driving scenario.

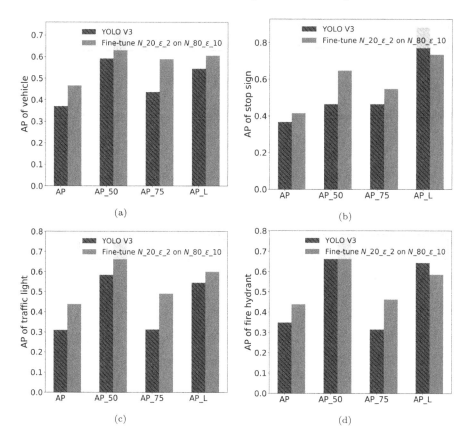

Fig. 9. Performance on autonomous driving related objects between pre-trained YOLO V3 and adversarially trained model. (a) AP on vehicle; (b) AP on stop sign; (c) AP on traffic lights; (d) AP on fire hydrant.

In particular, we use the same set adversarial examples with small ϵ and N as we did in Sect. 4.4. But we generate the set of B' based 5K images selected from super-category "vehicle" and "outdoor" [16]. Compare to the experiments (B' has 9,904 images) in Sect. 4.4, we save 49.52% on the adversarial training time for this autonomous driving scenario. We use the same "strong" examples ($N = 80, \epsilon = 10$) to test the models. Results are shown in Fig. 9. We pay more attention to the AP of objects related to autonomous driving. We observe some significant improvement in detecting vehicle and traffic light objects under the adversarial examples. Some visualization examples are provided in Fig. 11. We can see under some critical scenario such as crossing, our model outperforms the pre-trained YOLO V3.

4.6   Experiments on Other Attacks

We further study the robustness of our adversarially trained models against different types of adversarial examples. In particular, we test the performance of our models under two other attacks: 1. C&W attack [5] and 2. FGSM attack [7]. Like PGD, C&W attack is also an iterative attack while FGSM is a one-step attack. The results are shown in Fig. 10.

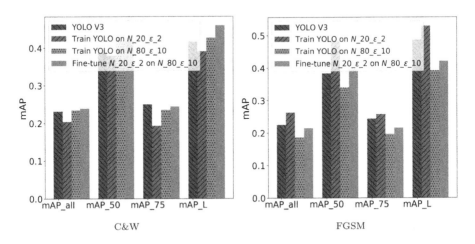

Fig. 10. Robustness on C&W and FGSM attacks.

We have some interesting observations. First, our models do not show obvious robustness on other attacks. Especially for C&W, our Algorithm 1 barely has any advantage, which also implies that model robustness might not be transferred between iterative adversarial examples. Second, the model trained with "weak" examples has the best performance against FGSM. One explanation is that the "weak" examples are close to the FGSM generated examples in the model output space, while fine-tuning by "strong" examples might increase the distance. Third, the pre-trained YOLO V3 is inherently more robust to C&W and FGSM examples (mAP around 0.24) than our PGD generated examples (mAP around 0.17).

YOLO V3   Our model

Fig. 11. Visual comparison between pre-trained YOLO V3 and our adversarially trained model on autonomous driving scenario.

5   Conclusion and Future Works

This work proposes a practical adversarial training to improve the robustness of state-of-art object detectors. We successfully improve the robustness of YOLO V3 on MS-COCO by utilizing our two-stage adversarial training. We then seek how to improve the model robustness on safety-critical scenarios more efficiently. Based on our experiment results, we revise the adversarial training by fine-tuning the first stage result using small but scenario-related datasets. And we verify the efficiency and robustness improvement on an autonomous driving scenario. For the time being, this work serves as a stepping stone towards efficient and effective robustness improvement for large-scale object detectors. But there are still many works to be done. For example, the extension of our algorithm on other network architectures such as Single Shot MultiBox Detector (SSD) or Region-Based Convolutional Neural Networks (R-CNN). A common problem with adversarial training is that it only works on the attack it is trained on. Our two-stage adversarial training partially serves as a regularizer which punishes the model for being overfitting. But how to fully adapt our adversarial training on other attacks such as FGSM is still a challenging future work.

References

1. Baidu: Baidu apollo. https://github.com/ApolloAuto/apollo
2. Bojarski, M., et al.: End to end learning for self-driving cars. arXiv e-prints arXiv:1604.07316, April 2016
3. Boudette, N.E., Vlasic, B.: Tesla self-driving system faulted by safety agency in crash. https://www.nytimes.com/2017/09/12/business/self-driving-cars.html
4. Cai, Z., Vasconcelos, N.: Cascade R-CNN: delving into high quality object detection. arXiv e-prints arXiv:1712.00726, December 2017
5. Carlini, N., Wagner, D.: Towards evaluating the robustness of neural networks. In: 2017 IEEE Symposium on Security and Privacy (SP), pp. 39–57. IEEE (2017)
6. Collobert, R., Weston, J.: A unified architecture for natural language processing: deep neural networks with multitask learning. In: Proceedings of the 25th International Conference on Machine Learning, ICML 2008, pp. 160–167. ACM, New York (2008). https://doi.org/10.1145/1390156.1390177
7. Goodfellow, I.J., Shlens, J., Szegedy, C.: Explaining and harnessing adversarial examples. arXiv e-prints arXiv:1412.6572, December 2014
8. Hinton, G., et al.: Deep neural networks for acoustic modeling in speech recognition: the shared views of four research groups. IEEE Signal Process. Mag. **29**(6), 82–97 (2012). https://doi.org/10.1109/MSP.2012.2205597
9. Huang, X., Kwiatkowska, M., Wang, S., Wu, M.: Safety verification of deep neural networks. arXiv e-prints arXiv:1610.06940, October 2016
10. Jia, Y., Lu, Y., Shen, J., Chen, Q.A., Zhong, Z., Wei, T.: Fooling detection alone is not enough: first adversarial attack against multiple object tracking. arXiv e-prints arXiv:1905.11026, May 2019
11. Kingma, D.P., Ba, J.: Adam: a method for stochastic optimization (2014). http://arxiv.org/abs/1412.6980, cite arxiv:1412.6980Comment. Published as a conference paper at the 3rd International Conference for Learning Representations, San Diego (2015)
12. Krizhevsky, A., Sutskever, I., Hinton, G.E.: ImageNet classification with deep convolutional neural networks. Commun. ACM **60**(6), 84–90 (2017). https://doi.org/10.1145/3065386. http://doi.acm.org/10.1145/3065386
13. Kurakin, A., Goodfellow, I., Bengio, S.: Adversarial examples in the physical world. arXiv e-prints arXiv:1607.02533, July 2016
14. Kurakin, A., Goodfellow, I., Bengio, S.: Adversarial machine learning at scale. arXiv e-prints arXiv:1611.01236, November 2016
15. Lecun, Y., Bottou, L., Bengio, Y., Haffner, P.: Gradient-based learning applied to document recognition. Proc. IEEE **86**(11), 2278–2324 (1998). https://doi.org/10.1109/5.726791
16. Lin, T.Y., et al.: Microsoft COCO: common objects in context. arXiv e-prints arXiv:1405.0312, May 2014
17. Lu, J., Sibai, H., Fabry, E., Forsyth, D.: NO need to worry about adversarial examples in object detection in autonomous vehicles. arXiv e-prints arXiv:1707.03501, July 2017
18. Madry, A., Makelov, A., Schmidt, L., Tsipras, D., Vladu, A.: Towards deep learning models resistant to adversarial attacks. arXiv e-prints arXiv:1706.06083, June 2017
19. Papernot, N., McDaniel, P., Goodfellow, I., Jha, S., Celik, Z.B., Swami, A.: Practical black-box attacks against machine learning. In: Proceedings of the 2017 ACM on Asia Conference on Computer and Communications Security (ASIA CCS 2017), Abu Dhabi, United Arab Emirates, pp. 506–519, April 2017. https://doi.org/10.1145/3052973.3053009. http://doi.acm.org/10.1145/3052973.3053009

20. Redmon, J., Divvala, S.K., Girshick, R.B., Farhadi, A.: You only look once: unified, real-time object detection. In: 2016 IEEE Conference on Computer Vision and Pattern Recognition, CVPR 2016, Las Vegas, NV, USA, 27–30 June 2016, pp. 779–788 (2016). https://doi.org/10.1109/CVPR.2016.91
21. Redmon, J., Farhadi, A.: Yolov3: an incremental improvement. arXiv (2018)
22. Ren, S., He, K., Girshick, R., Sun, J.: Faster R-CNN: towards real-time object detection with region proposal networks. In: Proceedings of the 28th International Conference on Neural Information Processing Systems - Volume 1, NIPS 2015, pp. 91–99. MIT Press, Cambridge (2015). http://dl.acm.org/citation.cfm?id=2969239.2969250
23. Szegedy, C., Ioffe, S., Vanhoucke, V., Alemi, A.: Inception-v4, Inception-ResNet and the impact of residual connections on learning. arXiv e-prints arXiv:1602.07261, February 2016
24. Szegedy, C., Zaremba, W., Sutskever, I., Bruna, J., Erhan, D., Goodfellow, I., Fergus, R.: Intriguing properties of neural networks. arXiv e-prints arXiv:1312.6199, December 2013
25. Xie, S., Girshick, R., Dollár, P., Tu, Z., He, K.: Aggregated residual transformations for deep neural networks. In: 2017 IEEE Conference on Computer Vision and Pattern Recognition (CVPR), pp. 5987–5995, July 2017. https://doi.org/10.1109/CVPR.2017.634
26. Zhang, H., Wang, J.: Towards adversarially robust object detection. In: The IEEE International Conference on Computer Vision (ICCV), October 2019
27. Zhang, W., Wu, X., Gao, J., Bao, D., Li, J., Zhou, X., et al.: Layer pruning for accelerating very deep neural networks. arXiv preprint arXiv:1910.12727 (2019)

Domain Generation Algorithm Detection Utilizing Model Hardening Through GAN-Generated Adversarial Examples

Nathaniel Gould[1]([✉]) [iD], Taishi Nishiyama[2], and Kazunori Kamiya[2]

[1] Georgia Institute of Technology, Atlanta, Georgia
ngould@gatech.edu
[2] NTT Secure Platform Laboratories, Tokyo, Japan
{taishi.nishiyama.pt,kazunori.kamiya.ew}@hco.ntt.co.jp

Abstract. Modern malware families often utilize Domain Generation Algorithms (DGAs) to register addresses for their Command and Control (C&C) servers. Instead of hardcoding the address of the C&C domain in the malware, DGAs are used to frequently change the address of the C&C server, causing static detection methods, such as blacklists, to be ineffective. In response, DGA detection methods have been proposed which attempt to detect these DGA-produced domains in live traffic.

Previous research has investigated using domains generated from a Generative Adversarial Network (GAN) to increase the ability of a detection model to detect unseen DGA variants. Building upon this concept, we test a similar experiment using an improved GAN and detection model. For the GAN, we train a Gradient Penalty Wasserstein GAN using benign domains as an input to produce set generated domains that are difficult to differentiate from real domains. The resulting set of domains have characteristics, such as character distribution, that more closely resemble real domains than sets produced in previous research. We then use these GAN-produced domains as additional examples of DGA domains and use them to augment the training set for a DGA detection model. While a feature engineering approach has been used in previous research, we use a deep learning, convolutional neural network and long short-term memory based detection model which had significantly higher hold-out detection rates for many DGA families. After training, we evaluate the model by comparing its detection rate on several holdout DGA families with GAN augmentation compared to the same model which used an augmented training set. This is shown to increase the detection rate of the classifier (at a standardized false positive rate) on certain DGA families. Further, unlike previous approaches, we conduct significance testing on the resulting detection rates to more accurately show the effect that adversarial hardening had on the model.

Keywords: Domain generating algorithm (DGA) · Botnet · Malware · Deep learning · Generative Adversarial Network (GAN)

© Springer Nature Switzerland AG 2020
G. Wang et al. (Eds.): MLHat 2020, CCIS 1271, pp. 84–101, 2020.
https://doi.org/10.1007/978-3-030-59621-7_5

1   Introduction

Modern botnet malware families frequently utilize centralized command and control (C&C) servers to communicate with the owner of the botnet, the botmaster. This communication could potentially involve performing denial-of-service attacks [1], sending spam [13], stealing data, and activating ransomware. To perform these functions, however, the malware needs to know the address of a C&C server. The simple approach, hardcoding the domain name in the malware directly, leaves the communication channel vulnerable, as the C&C server may eventually be identified and taken down. To avoid this, malware designers started implementing domain generation algorithms (DGAs) to frequently change the address of their C&C server. These DGAs are able to generate a large number of pseudo random domain names based on an initial seed [15]. The botmaster can then register some of these domains to host their C&C servers. A bot can then generate and attempt to connect with the same list of possible domains until it establishes a connection with a C&C server. Through this process, even if a C&C server is identified and shutdown by authorities or cybersecurity companies, attackers can simply register a new address for their C&C server to bring their botnet back online.

To detect these algorithmically generated domains (AGDs) in live traffic, two approaches have been primarily used: feature engineering using traditional machine learning algorithms and deep learning based algorithms.

Feature engineering involves manually extracting useful information about the domain to use as inputs for a machine learning algorithm, such as random forest. As an example, some DGA families have a high degree of randomness due to being produced from a random seed. This means that character entropy could be a useful feature to use to identify domains from more random DGAs. Another possible feature could be domain length, as DGAs tend to produce domains that are on average longer than legitimate domains. However, this strategy can leave the model vulnerable to adversarial tuning, as attackers can alter their DGA to avoid being detected by certain features, such as creating domains from a smaller pool of possible characters to reduce the entropy of the domains produced, or setting a shorter max length when producing domains.

In contrast, deep learning based algorithms use a series of processing layers to extract features from a raw input, in this case the characters of each domain name. Since there are no easily calculable features, it can be more difficult to know how a DGA has to be tuned in order to bypass the detection model. Additionally, Sidi et al. [18] showed that a deep learning classifier was more resistant to black box attacks than a feature engineering based random forest detection model. In terms of being used as a detection model, deep learning based classifiers have been shown to achieve higher detection rates when using domain strings as inputs compared to traditional machine learning models such as linear regression and random forest [22].

Previous works have proposed the idea of using adversarial augmentation of the training dataset to harden machine learning based classifiers [9]. This idea was applied to the concept of DGA detection by Anderson et al. [2], who used a generative adversarial network (GAN), called DeepDGA, to generate DGA domains that were hard to differentiate from legitimate domains. They found that adding these domains to the training set of a random forest model could improve the model's ability to detect new DGA variants. In this model, the generator takes random noise as an input and transforms it into a domain name (without a top level domain). Correspondingly, the discriminator attempts to differentiate between the domains produced by the generator and real domains. By iteratively training these models together, the generator learns to produce domains that are increasingly difficult to detect by the discriminator and the discriminator learns to be able to better differentiate the real and artificial domains. After training, the generator is able to produce domains that are similar in appearance to benign domains. The generator was then used to create a set of DGA domains that were added to the training set of a random forest DGA detection model, which was shown to have a higher detection rate on many unseen DGA families when compared to an unaugmented control model.

Expanding on this idea, we further test the effectiveness of using GANs to harden an AGD detection model. Rather than performing pre-training on an autoencoder, we use a more complex GAN where all layers of the network are trainable, increasing the learning capacity of the network during training. We also implement a Wasserstein loss function with a gradient penalty term [5] to increase the stability and convergence of the GAN. Through these methods, we were able to generate domains that were more similar to benign domains than those achieved in previous work. Further, to test model hardening, we used a deep learning model as our detection model rather than random forest due to deep learning based classification models being shown to have better detection rates than traditional machine learning models in previous research [22]. This allowed our model to achieve higher detection rates for many DGA families when compared to the DeepDGA detection model [2].

In summary, contributions of this paper include:

- We propose a new domain generation approach using a Wasserstein GAN with a gradient penalty that was able to produce a set of domains more similar to real domains than previous approaches.
- We explore how augmenting affects the detection rate (at a standardized false positive rate) of a convolutional neural network (CNN) and long short-term memory (LSTM) classifier which has a higher detection rate of DGA domains than the feature engineering model used in previous research.
- We use confidence testing to determine the significance of detection rate changes caused by augmentation for each DGA family to account for the increased variance in detection rate caused by leave one out validation.

2   Related Works

In previous works, DGA domains have been shown to be detectable by manually crafted domain name features as inputs into a supervised learning model, commonly random forest [3,17]. Previously used features include character entropy,

URL length, the presence of non-existent domain errors in the network [3], vowel to consonant ratio, as well as character n-grams [12]. Disadvantages of this type of approach include the difficulty of manually extracting features, as well as being more vulnerable to adversarial attacks if the detection model is leaked, or if the attacker uses a more sophisticated DGA that is not as detectable by the chosen features [14].

Deep learning methods have also been shown to be effective at detecting DGA domains. Vinayakumar et al. [19] and Yu et al. [22] compared various character-level deep learning model architectures by training and testing each model on the same subsets of data. From their results, models which used LSTM and/or CNN layers were seen to be the most effective and were able to achieve a higher accuracy compared to feature engineering based models. In both studies, the Endgame model [21] which used an LSTM, was shown to frequently have one of the highest detection rates across several test datasets. Similarly, in tests performed by Kumar et al. [11], models that used CNN-LSTM architectures were shown to have the highest F1 and AUC scores. Based on these results, we implemented a model which used CNN layers in parallel followed by a LSTM layer. Additionally, all the deep learning models were shown to have higher detection rates than traditional machine learning methods using feature engineering like random forest. In our testing, adding a fully connected layer after the LSTM layer was observed to increase the performance of the model.

3 Background

3.1 Botnets and Domain Generation Algorithms

A botnet is a collection of internet-enabled devices (bots) that have been infected with malware that allows them to be controlled by an attacker. Common attacks carried out by botnets include performing denial-of-service attacks [1], sending spam [13], stealing data, and activating ransomware. To perform these actions, a botmaster uses C&C servers that act as rendezvous points for communication with their bots. Due to their high importance in the functioning of the botnet, malware often utilize a DGA to pseudo-randomly generate a large number of new domain names starting from a seed value. Sample domains from DGAs used in this paper are shown in Table 1. Out of these domains, a few may be registered as addresses for a C&C server. A bot can then use the same seed to generate an identical list of domain names as the attacker. The bot will then attempt to contact each domain until it successfully connects with a C&C server. This procedure causes static methods, such as blacklisting, to be ineffective, allowing botmasters to evade investigations and shutdowns by authorities and security companies [19]. For these reasons, the real time detection of DGA domains is crucial to reduce the potential damage that can be caused by botnets.

3.2 Generative Adversarial Networks

GANs are a deep learning framework where two competing models, a generator and discriminator, compete in a series of adversarial rounds. As proposed by

Table 1. Example domains from several DGA families

DGA	Sample 1	Sample 2
Cryptolocker	`ptlwqfsfvhxlaxw.com`	`wwcdhdhijsfsuyr.net`
Corebot	`y4c2or7pwly6s2a.ddns.net`	`m6uto0ab3j3hurc.ddns.net`
Dircrypt	`rfkqyuqfjkxyqvnrtys.com`	`fpdadtgazqf.com`
Fobber	`drohppbkxj.net`	`gbjtyyhrhk.net`
Kraken	`unqtrauoe.com`	`bwmnqaa.cc`
Locky_v2	`libnxmsfagoiknjhp.ru`	`astewdf.info`
Nymaim	`ekbvbueuywl.info`	`wyvtdjhcg.cc`
Padcrypt	`dfckebllebbmnoon.com`	`bombmbcmmkmfddng.de`
Pykspa	`vlwior.net`	`xunynqnaz.info`
Qakbot	`gsunghpcfium.org`	`rgjnpumyluz.info`
Ramdo	`kusumyekqaaskcqw.org`	`skkikukwuauawigs.org`
Ramnit	`prklqkkwhgpshiej.com`	`rvcophrldijwrnldbqj.com`
Shiotob	`dduub92cik.net`	`fzwrzifvtl.com`
Simda	`gatyfus.com`	`lyvyxor.com`
Symmi	`qiafsuqocodovel.ddns.net`	`tiegabactuleul.ddns.net`

Goodfellow et al. [8], a generative model transforms low-dimensional noise into samples that resemble real data. To do this, the generator is trained alongside a discriminator network, which attempts to differentiate samples of real data from samples created by the generator. The discriminator provides feedback to the generator which it uses to tune its weights to produce samples that the discriminator considers to be real. Through iterative application of the objective function over a series of training rounds, the performance of both models increases ideally until the generator is able to produce real enough samples to completely confuse the discriminator.

3.3 Wasserstein GAN

GAN training as originally proposed [8] has been shown to have difficulty with maintaining convergence between the generator and discriminator models [5]. This is often caused by the real and generated distributions being disjoint which can result in the gradients being received by the generator to be unstable or vanish towards zero.

Due to the simultaneous training of the generator and discriminator through a zero-sum game, stable training requires both models to have similar abilities. When training, the discriminator can often quickly learn the difference between real and generated domains, which may cause the two distributions to become disjoint, causing the generator to provide no informative gradient information during back propagation. This causes the generator to no longer improve significantly during training, thus making the model fail to converge.

To help reduce the impact of these problems, Wasserstein GAN was proposed which uses an earth-mover distance as its objective function [5]. Unlike the objective function used in the original GAN implementation, Wasserstein loss can still give an accurate distance measurement by being differentiable almost everywhere, even when the two distributions are disjoint. Additionally, rather than outputting a probability of being malicious, WGAN's discriminator acts more like a critic and outputs an unbound score representing the "realness" of the input. This makes it possible for the model to still learn even when the generator is performing poorly. For WGAN, the competing generator and discriminator implement the minmax function for a given data instance x:

$$\min_{G}\max_{D\in\mathcal{D}} \mathbb{E}_{x\sim\mathbb{P}_r}[D(x)] - \mathbb{E}_{\tilde{x}\sim\mathbb{P}_g}[D(\tilde{x})] \tag{1}$$

- $\mathbb{P}_r$ is the distribution over all real data.
- $\mathbb{E}_{x\sim\mathbb{P}_r}$ is the expected value over all real data instances.
- $D(x)$ is the discriminator's estimate of the probability that the real data instance x is real.
- $\mathbb{P}_g$ is the generator's distribution over all fake data.
- $\mathbb{E}_{\tilde{x}\sim\mathbb{P}_g}$ is the expected value over all generated (fake) instances.
- $D(\tilde{x})$ is the discriminator's estimate that the fake instance $\tilde{x}$ is real.

3.4   Lipschitz Continuity Constant

A function is known to be Lipschitz continuous if there exists some real constant value $L \geq 0$ such that for the inputs, x and y, and the outputs, $f(y)$ and $f(x)$ the relationship:

$$\|f(y) - f(x)))\| \leq L\|y - x\|, \forall x, y \in \mathbb{R}^n \tag{2}$$

holds true. The Lipschitz continuity enforces that there is a linear relationship between the inputs and outputs to a function. Satisfying the Lipschitz continuity imposes that the function cannot grow faster than linearly and guarantees the trend that the generated distribution gets closer to the real distribution every step.

3.5   Gradient Penalty Wasserstein GAN

For WGAN, the Lipschitz property is enforced by clipping layer weights to chosen min/max values which allow WGAN to achieve both more stability and higher quality results than the standard GAN network. However, this approach can still fail to converge due to weight clipping reducing the function space to a proper subset of all Lipschitz functions, which could prevent the model from achieving the optimal critic if this subset does not include the optimum.

Instead of clipping weights, Wasserstein GAN Gradient Penalty (WGAN-GP) penalizes the deviation of the critic's gradient norm from 1 for random samples

$\hat{x} \sim \mathbb{P}_{\hat{x}}$, softly enforcing that the objective function is Lipschitz-1. $\mathbb{P}_{\hat{x}}$ represents sampling uniformly along straight lines between pairs of points that are sampled from the data distribution $\mathbb{P}_r$ and the generator distribution $\mathbb{P}_g$. This is done due to the optimal critic containing straight lines with a gradient norm of 1 between coupled points from $\mathbb{P}_r$ and $\mathbb{P}_g$ [9]. This method has been shown to increase the stability of training, improving the performance of the model during later rounds of training compared to models which utilize weight clipping [9]. Additionally, WGAN-GP needs less hyperparameter tuning to perform effectively due to it not having to set weight clipping cutoffs. The objective function for WGAN-GP is defined as:

$$L = \underbrace{\mathbb{E}_{\tilde{x} \sim \mathbb{P}_g}[D(\tilde{x})] - \mathbb{E}_{x \sim \mathbb{P}_r}[D(x)]}_{critic\ loss} + \underbrace{\lambda \mathbb{E}_{\hat{x} \sim \mathbb{P}_{\hat{x}}}[(\|\nabla_{\hat{x}} D(\hat{x})\|_2 - 1)^2]}_{gradient\ penealty} \qquad (3)$$

λ is a hyperparameter which represents a Lagrange multiplier. The Wasserstein critic loss is penalized by the norm gradient with respect to the input of the critic to softly enforce the function to be Lipschitz-1. $P_{\hat{x}}$ denotes the distribution of samples created by interpolating pairs from the distributions P_r and P_g.

3.6   Recurrent Neural Networks

Recurrent neural networks (RNN) are a type of deep learning network that incorporate contextual information in their mapping from input to output, allowing the network to retain information about previous inputs. This allows the network to have the capacity to find temporal relationships between sequential tokens in the input. This makes RNNs excel at processing textual data due to it being naturally sequential, which has been shown in previous work [6,10,21,22]. Using a RNN in our model allows it to have additional contextual information about the inputted domain such as character location and which characters are located around that character's position. A LSTM is a variant of RNN used due to its abilities to handle long term dependencies compared to standard RNNs, where loss function gradients can begin to decay exponentially [7]. For our purposes, using a LSTM allows the network to know the order that characters appear in the domain. Since we use padding to make each imputed domain the same length, the network is also able to indirectly know the length of a domain by knowing the locations of these padding characters.

3.7   Convolutional Neural Networks

Convolutional neural networks (CNN) are a type of deep learning network that generates features by applying filters over its inputs to recognize patterns. Additional layers allow the network to have the capacity to recognize more complex relationships in the data. This has allowed CNNs to be successful in image recognition tasks using 2D convolution layers, as well as more recently, natural language processing by using 1D filters over an input of characters [20]. By using a CNN, a

DGA detection model has the capacity to recognize patterns present in the groupings of characters in the domain. This is useful for detection if some character groupings are significantly more or less common in DGA or benign domains.

4   Proposed Architecture

4.1   GAN Discriminator Input Formatting

While GANs have previously shown to be successful at generating continuous outputs such as pixel values to create an image, GANs often struggle with generating discrete outputs. Having distinct outputs makes the small updates from back propagation ineffective due to there being no intermediate values in between the discrete outputs, in this case valid domain characters. To solve this problem a softmax activation is used for the output layer of the generator. This causes the generator to output 63 vectors of size 38 where each vector represents a character position for a domain and each vector is a stochastic vector which represents the probability of each possible discrete domain character occurring there. Due to these output probabilities being continuous, the output of the generator can be updated though gradient descent during back propagation. To generate domains from the generator after training, a weighted sample or argmax can be taken to choose a character for each possible position. To make real inputs to the discriminator have the same shape as the output of the generator, real samples were extended to have a length of 63 by adding padding characters. Each character in the domain was then converted to a one-hot vector of size 38 for each possible discrete domain character. This made each domain have the same shape (63×38) as the generator.

4.2   GAN Model

The GAN model architecture was based on the GAN model used in DeepDGA. The discriminator of the GAN was also created to be similar to previous successful DGA detection models [22] where a LSTM and parallel CNN layer model was able to achieve one of the highest accuracies compared to other deep learning detection models. The generator was chosen to have the same layers as the discriminator to prevent one network from overpowering the other which would make it more likely that the GAN would fail to converge [4].

For the objective function of the GAN, we implement the WGAN-GP function [9] due to its higher stability and convergence compared to WGAN and the originally proposed GAN objective function.

The discriminator of the GAN first uses parallel convolution layers of filter sizes 2 and 3 over the domain. The merged output is then passed to an LSTM layer, which is then passed into a fully connected layer. A dropout layer is used between the LSTM and fully connected layer which causes some nodes to be excluded during training. This breaks up the complex co-adaptations that may be learned by the network during training, which could potentially result in overfitting. Dropout is only used while training the network and it is not used when creating domains with the generator. The final output is expressed by a linear activation function which allows the network to output an unbound score to be used as the critic's output for the Wasserstein loss function.

The generating portion of the GAN uses the same layer structure as the discriminator, but in reverse, which was shown to be successful when creating the DeepDGA model. It is useful to have the generator and discriminator models use the same layers so one model can not easily overpower the other, which could lead to increased instability during training.

An overview of the architecture for the GAN model can be seen in Fig. 1.

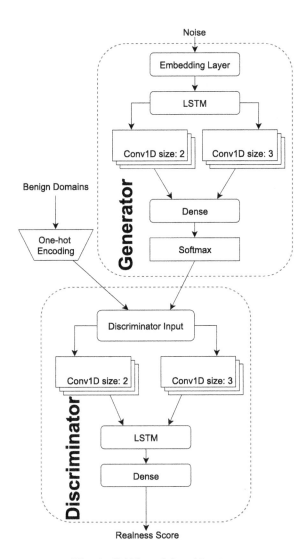

Fig. 1. GAN model architecture

4.3   AGD Detection Model

To test the effectiveness of augmentation using GAN-generated domains, a deep learning DGA detection model was created based on their layer architecture used by the critic in the GAN model. However, instead of acting like a critic by using a linear output, a sigmoid output was used to represent the confidence that an input is an AGD. Additionally, an embedding layer was used rather than one-hot encoding. Adam was used as the optimization function.

5   Experiment Setup

5.1   Benign Domain Set

Examples of real domains were obtained from the Tranco top one million dataset. The Tranco dataset is designed to be used as a whitelist for research, so it has less daily fluctuations than other popular datasets (Alexa[1], Umbrella[2], Majesti[3]). Additionally, malicious sites, such as those hosting malware or used for phishing, have been shown to occur in many other popular top domain lists [16]. These domains could lead to errors when they are used as an example of a benign domain, so known malicious sites are removed from the Tranco rankings. By removing these types of domains, the Tranco dataset functions better for our purpose as a whitelist of benign examples.

5.2   Algorithmically Generated Domain Set

The set of AGDs used was generated by running Python implementations of reverse engineered DGAs. Unlike live DGA feeds, this allowed a sufficient number of domains to be generated for training and testing for each DGA family.

Dictionary-based DGAs were not included in this set due to their extremely low detection rate by character level LSTM and CNN models, as well as their high collision rate with registered domains. For example, 74.39% of `Suppobox` AGDs and 40.0% of `Matsnu` AGDs (both wordlist-based DGAs) collide with existing domains [15]. In several previous works, dictionary-based DGAs have often been seen to be almost undetectable by character-based deep learning approaches. This is seen in the detection model created by Woodbridge et al. [21] where the detection rate for dictionary AGD is very low, illustrating that character-based classifiers have difficulty differentiating between real and dictionary-produced domains due to their similar character groupings. Previous deep learning models that have been able to detect dictionary DGAs usually have enough examples of the DGA in their training set to memorize the words in the dictionary [21].

To generate the set of AGDs, known hard-coded seeds or the current date (for time-seeded DGAs) were used to generate 10,000 domains for each DGA.

---

[1] https://www.alexa.com/topsites.

[2] https://docs.umbrella.com/investigate-api/docs/top-million-domains.

[3] https://majestic.com/reports/majestic-million.

5.3 GAN Generated Samples

For training the GAN, Adam was chosen as the optimizer. While WGAN has been shown to not perform well using optimizers with momentum and consequently used RMSprop [5], WGAN-GP has been shown to converge faster with the momentum-based Adam optimizer than RMSprop on test datasets [9]. Due to this, Adam was chosen as the optimizer for the GAN model. Additionally, the value for the Lagrange multiplier hyperparameter of the WGAN-GP objective function was set to a value of 10, which has been shown to be successful on various test datasets [9].

Samples were generated using the trained generator from the GAN model by inputting noise made of 63 numbers that had possible values of 0 to 37, representing the 38 valid second level domain characters (a–z, 0–9, hyphen, and a padding character so all domains would have a length of 63). To create domains from the 63 character output, the generated domain was cut after the first appearance of a padding character. To reduce the amount of collisions with real domains, generated domains with a resulting length of less than five characters were cut from the dataset.

Both the GAN model and DGA detection model were implemented with Keras using the TensorFlow 2.0 beta.

5.4 Adversarial Data Augmentation

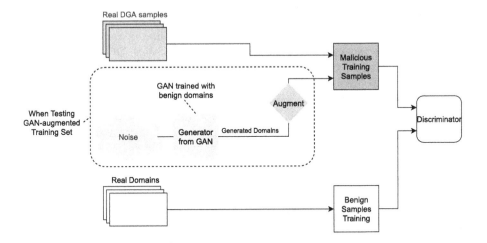

Fig. 2. Training data augmentation process

Many previously proposed DGA detection algorithms use a daily feed for their AGD set, such as the live Bambenek Consulting feed[4] [22]. These domains are

---

[4] https://osint.bambenekconsulting.com/feeds/.

then split into a training and testing set where domains from the same DGA family are present in both the training and testing subsets. However this setup does not measure the ability of the model to detect new DGA variants. Thus, to simulate a more realistic AGD detection environment, the detection model was evaluated on its accuracy on DGA families not present in the training set. This was performed by entirely removing one of the DGA families to be used as a testing set using hold-out validation. Due to the increased detection rate variance caused by hold-out validation, the GAN augmented and the control model were trained 10 times for each hold-out DGA family. The true positive rate (TPR) was measured when the false positive rate was set to 0.01 to maintain consistency across models. For each trained model, the same set of 150,000 benign domains was used along with the same set of AGDs. The benign domains were randomly sampled from the Tranco set of one million domains for each round, however both models for each training round used the same subset of sampled domains. The 10 detection rates were then used to perform a t-test between the distributions to determine if the change in detection rate between the control and GAN augmented models was statistically significant. An overview of data augmentation process used is illustrated in Fig. 2.

5.5 Evaluation Metrics

To measure the effectiveness of the augmented training despite variances in accuracy between rounds, a paired t-test was performed on the detection rate difference between the augmented and unaugmented training data. The t-test is calculated by finding the relationship between the signal strength $\bar{d}$ compared to the sample's noise $s/\sqrt{n}$ where $\bar{d}$ and s are the mean and standard deviation of the differences between the observed accuracies in the model, respectively. n is the size of d. The t-score can then be found through the equation:

$$t = \frac{\bar{d}}{s/\sqrt{n}} \tag{4}$$

The t-score can then be used to find the p-value, which measures the significance of the change in detection rate between the GAN augmented and control models. The resulting p-value represents the likelihood of the null hypothesis, in this case the likelihood that the GAN TPR and control TPR could have been derived from the same normal distribution. A small p-value indicates that there is little confidence in the null hypothesis being true, indicating that there is a significant difference between the GAN and control TPRs.

6 Results

6.1 GAN Domain Generation

As seen in Fig. 3, the lengths of produced domains were distributed similarly to benign domains (not including the shorter domains which were cut from the generated dataset). Additionally, the domains produced followed a character distribution that was similar to the character distribution of benign domains as seen in Fig. 4. As a result, the domains produced were often pronounceable by containing common letter combinations found in the real domain set. Overall, the GAN produced domain set appear to be more similar to the benign set than those produced through the GAN of DeepDGA in Fig. 5 [2]. For instance, domains produced by DeepDGA had an occurrence rate of 0.18 for the character "e" compared to the real occurrence rate of 0.10 in the Alexa dataset that was used as examples for non-AGDs. The hyphen symbol "-" also had an occurrence rate of 0.07 in DeepDGA domains where it occurred at a rate >0.01 in real domains [2] (Table 2).

Table 2. A random sample of GAN-generated domains

khecest	oondvilamaehatyart	jeltitisoras
muitenich	hkind	dicgoagi
oleswert	wtuschich	upheaminulel
dretodee	moglorrilit	wartole
derilasnetansi	thmososs	gstov
dhamow	kanteerete	pentare
seblohercranje	hcrig	bayhtedpe
sjite	bojalhoslt	emewsals
tershiffan	mojrestkil	oopbloebiglasont

The generator of the trained GAN was used to produce 10,000 new domains from random noise which are used as adversarial examples of generated domains to augment the training set of a DGA detection model.

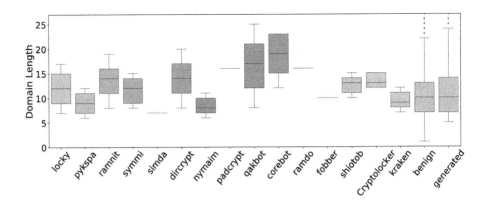

Fig. 3. Domain length distributions for DGA, benign, and GAN-produced domains

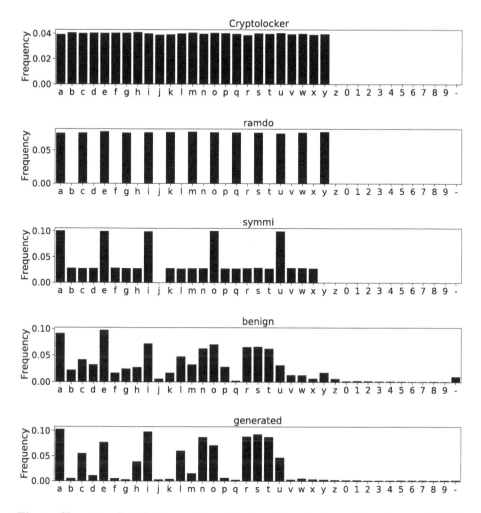

Fig. 4. Character distributions of Cryptolocker, Ramdo, Symmi, benign, and GAN-generated domains

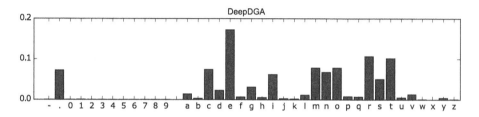

Fig. 5. Character distribution of the domain set produced by the DeepDGA GAN [2]

6.2   DGA Detection Model

Due to the volatility of the TPR between tests using the same model with shuffled data, a 0.95 confidence level was used as the threshold for a two sample paired t-test to determine if the results were statistically significant. In Table 3, accuracy differences with at least 95% confidence are bolded.

The augmented model was seen to improve the detection rate on DGA families that had a high TPR rate of approximately 0.95 for both the control and augmented model. Inversely, the GAN augmented model had a lower detection rate on hard to detect DGAs when compared to the unaugmented model. The detection rates for Cryptolocker, Padcrypt, Ramdo, and Symmi saw significant improvements over the control model.

Table 3. Detection rate of hold-out DGA families (FPR = 0.01)

DGA	Baseline TPR	GAN TPR	p-value (t-test)
Cryptolocker	0.968	**0.978**	**0.028**
Corebot	0.277	0.287	0.487
Dircrypt	0.958	0.956	0.313
Fobber	0.932	0.936	0.625
Kraken	0.872	0.826	0.078
Locky	0.889	0.877	0.055
Nymaim	**0.679**	0.644	**0.021**
Padcrypt	0.911	**0.953**	**0.003**
Pykspa	**0.708**	0.676	**0.004**
Qakbot	0.965	0.967	0.233
Ramdo	0.972	**0.988**	**0.012**
Ramnit	0.943	0.944	0.900
Shiotob	0.488	0.475	0.201
Simda	0.284	0.231	0.056
Symmi	0.331	**0.407**	**0.021**

Despite the control outperforming the GAN augmented model for many low detection rate families, the data augmentation did improve the detection rate for Symmi, which alternates between constants and vowels to produce pronounceable-looking domains. Due to this generation formula, Symmi can be hard to detect, even when a model has samples of it in its training set. The increase in detection rate is likely due to the increased similarity of domain character occurrences used in Symmi and GAN domains. As can be seen in Fig. 4 where both Symmi and the GAN-generated domains have similarly-high vowel usage.

When compared to the detection model used in DeepDGA [2] (which also measured the TPR at FPR = 0.01), our detection model was able to achieve much higher base detection rates for many DGA families. For example, our augmented model had a TPR of 0.978 for `Cryptolocker` compared to the TPR of 0.88 for the DeepDGA model. We see similar accuracy increases for `Dircrypt`, `Qakbot`, `Locky`, `Kraken`, and `Ramdo`. We only observe significant decreases in accuracy for `Corebot` and `Simda`, as well as a small decrease for `Pykspa`. While some variation may be attributed to differences in the dataset used, based on previous research, the observed accuracy differences are most likely due to the CNN and LSTM detection model we used compared to the random forest model used in DeepDGA [22].

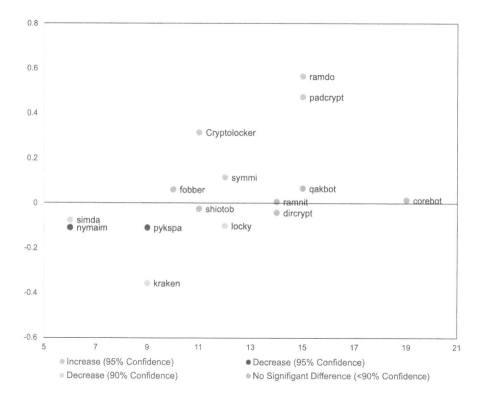

Fig. 6. Length and error rate reduction of DGA families by the GAN-augmented DGA detection model

From the results on the families tested, it appears that the GAN augmented model had lower accuracies than the control for DGA families that produce shorter domain names. Out of the five domains that had lower accuracy for the augmented model, four of them had an average length of less than ten characters. Conversely, all families with improved accuracy with the augmented model had more than eleven characters. Thus, GAN augmentation appears to be more successful on DGAs that produce longer domains. This relationship can be observed when the average length of domains for each DGA is plotted against the ratio of error rates (the GAN augmented rate of misclassification divided by the control rate of misclassification) in Fig. 6. This view gives a larger difference in weight to families that had a high base-classification rate. One possible explanation for this decrease in detection rate is that shorter domains have less features generated by filtering through the model layers. Therefore, shorter domains may be naturally more likely to conflict and thus appear similar to real domains.

7   Conclusion

We have demonstrated the ability of using an LSTM and CNN network to generate hard-to-classify domains by using a generative adversarial network. Additionally we have shown that our proposed method results in improved performance compared to previously proposed methods for the DeepDGA model [2]. First, we show that utilizing a Wasserstein GAN with a gradient penalty can produce more varied samples that have characteristics more similar to that of real domains. Second, we show that our tested CNN and LSTM model is able to achieve significantly higher accuracies after augmentation than the accuracies achieved through the random forest model used in DeepDGA. Third, we use significance testing to account for the increased variation of hold-out family testing to increase the confidence of our results. Overall, we also confirm the idea of adversarial data augmentation that was proposed for the DeepDGA model, and show that augmentation can result in higher detection rates for a deep learning based DGA detection model.

References

1. Alomari, E., Manickam, S., Gupta, B., Karuppayah, S., Alfaris, R.: Botnet-based distributed denial of service (DDoS) attacks on web servers: classification and art. arXiv preprint arXiv:1208.0403 (2012)
2. Anderson, H.S., Woodbridge, J., Filar, B.: DeepDGA: adversarially-tuned domain generation and detection. In: Proceedings of the 2016 ACM Workshop on Artificial Intelligence and Security, pp. 13–21 (2016)
3. Antonakakis, M., et al.: From throw-away traffic to bots: detecting the rise of DGA-based malware. In: Presented as part of the 21st {USENIX} Security Symposium ({USENIX} Security 2012), pp. 491–506 (2012)
4. Arjovsky, M., Bottou, L.: Towards principled methods for training generative adversarial networks. arXiv preprint arXiv:1701.04862 (2017)
5. Arjovsky, M., Chintala, S., Bottou, L.: Wasserstein GAN. arXiv preprint arXiv:1701.07875 (2017)
6. Bengio, Y., Boulanger-Lewandowski, N., Pascanu, R.: Advances in optimizing recurrent networks. In: 2013 IEEE International Conference on Acoustics, Speech and Signal Processing, pp. 8624–8628. IEEE (2013)
7. Gers, F.A., Schmidhuber, J., Cummins, F.: Learning to forget: continual prediction with LSTM. Neural Comput. **12**, 2451–2471 (1999)
8. Goodfellow, I., et al.: Generative adversarial nets. In: Advances in Neural Information Processing Systems, pp. 2672–2680 (2014)

9. Goodfellow, I.J., Shlens, J., Szegedy, C.: Explaining and harnessing adversarial examples. arXiv preprint arXiv:1412.6572 (2014)
10. Kim, Y., Jernite, Y., Sontag, D., Rush, A.: Character-aware neural language models. arXiv preprint arXiv:1508.06615 (2016)
11. Kumar, A.D., et al.: Enhanced domain generating algorithm detection based on deep neural networks. In: Alazab, M., Tang, M.J. (eds.) Deep Learning Applications for Cyber Security. ASTSA, pp. 151–173. Springer, Cham (2019). https://doi.org/10.1007/978-3-030-13057-2_7
12. Mac, H., Tran, D., Tong, V., Nguyen, L.G., Tran, H.A.: DGA botnet detection using supervised learning methods. In: Proceedings of the Eighth International Symposium on Information and Communication Technology, pp. 211–218 (2017)
13. Pathak, A., Qian, F., Hu, Y.C., Mao, Z.M., Ranjan, S.: Botnet spam campaigns can be long lasting: evidence, implications, and analysis. ACM SIGMETRICS Perform. Eval. Rev. **37**(1), 13–24 (2009)
14. Peck, J., et al.: CharBot: a simple and effective method for evading DGA classifiers. IEEE Access **7**, 91759–91771 (2019)
15. Plohmann, D., Yakdan, K., Klatt, M., Bader, J., Gerhards-Padilla, E.: A comprehensive measurement study of domain generating malware. In: 25th {USENIX} Security Symposium ({USENIX} Security 2016), pp. 263–278 (2016)
16. Pochat, V.L., Van Goethem, T., Tajalizadehkhoob, S., Korczyński, M., Joosen, W.: Tranco: a research-oriented top sites ranking hardened against manipulation. arXiv preprint arXiv:1806.01156 (2018)
17. Schiavoni, S., Maggi, F., Cavallaro, L., Zanero, S.: Phoenix: DGA-based botnet tracking and intelligence. In: Dietrich, S. (ed.) DIMVA 2014. LNCS, vol. 8550, pp. 192–211. Springer, Cham (2014). https://doi.org/10.1007/978-3-319-08509-8_11
18. Sidi, L., Nadler, A., Shabtai, A.: MaskDGA: a black-box evasion technique against DGA classifiers and adversarial defenses. arXiv preprint arXiv:1902.08909 (2019)
19. Vinayakumar, R., Soman, K.P., Poornachandran, P., Alazab, M., Jolfaei, A.: DBD: deep learning DGA-based botnet detection. In: Alazab, M., Tang, M.J. (eds.) Deep Learning Applications for Cyber Security. ASTSA, pp. 127–149. Springer, Cham (2019). https://doi.org/10.1007/978-3-030-13057-2_6
20. Vosoughi, S., Vijayaraghavan, P., Roy, D.: Tweet2Vec: learning tweet embeddings using character-level CNN-LSTM encoder-decoder. In: Proceedings of the 39th International ACM SIGIR Conference on Research and Development in Information Retrieval, pp. 1041–1044 (2016)
21. Woodbridge, J., Anderson, H.S., Ahuja, A., Grant, D.: Predicting domain generation algorithms with long short-term memory networks. arXiv preprint arXiv:1611.00791 (2016)
22. Yu, B., Pan, J., Hu, J., Nascimento, A., De Cock, M.: Character level based detection of DGA domain names. In: 2018 International Joint Conference on Neural Networks (IJCNN), pp. 1–8. IEEE (2018)

Threats on Networks

Toward Explainable and Adaptable Detection and Classification of Distributed Denial-of-Service Attacks

Yebo Feng$^{(\boxtimes)}$ and Jun Li

University of Oregon, Eugene, OR 97403, USA
{yebof,lijun}@cs.uoregon.edu

Abstract. By attacking (e.g., flooding) the bandwidth or resources of a victim (e.g., a web server) on the Internet from multiple compromised systems (e.g., a botnet), distributed Denial-of-Service (DDoS) attacks disrupt the services of the victim and make it unavailable to its legitimate users. Albeit studied many years already, the detection of DDoS attacks remains a troubling problem. In this paper, we propose a new, learning-based DDoS detection and classification method that is both explainable and adaptable. This method first utilizes a modified k-nearest neighbors (KNN) algorithm to detect DDoS attacks and then uses risk degree sorting with grids to classify traffic at a fine granularity. It uses a k-dimensional tree to partition the searching space that significantly improves its efficiency and shortens KNN query times. Moreover, compared with the previous DDoS detection and classification approaches, along with the detection results this method further generates risk profiles that provides users with interpretability for filtering DDoS traffic. Additionally, this method does not need to retrain the detection model in order to make it fit in a new network environment. Users can leverage a variety of prior knowledge to evolve the model. We evaluated this approach in both simulated environments and the real world, which shows that our approach is both effective and efficient. It achieves a 98.4% accuracy in detecting DDoS attacks with a delay of around 5 s.

Keywords: Distributed Denial-of-Service (DDoS) · DDoS detection · Anomaly detection · Machine learning · K-nearest neighbors (KNN)

1 Introduction

Distributed denial-of-service attacks (DDoS attacks) pose a severe security problem on today's Internet and can make specific servers, network infrastructures, or applications unavailable to their users. They typically operate by overwhelming the targeted machine or network resource with excessive requests, therefore preventing legitimate requests from being fulfilled [4]. Cisco released a white paper in March 2020 and indicated that the frequency of DDoS attacks had increased more than 2.5 times over the last three years. Moreover, the average

© Springer Nature Switzerland AG 2020
G. Wang et al. (Eds.): MLHat 2020, CCIS 1271, pp. 105–121, 2020.
https://doi.org/10.1007/978-3-030-59621-7_6

size of DDoS attacks is increasing steadily and approaching 1 Gbps, enough to paralyze most websites thoroughly [7].

Key to effectively preventing and mitigating DDoS attacks is prompt and accurate DDoS detection. Decades of research and industry efforts have led to a myriad of DDoS detection and classification approaches. In the beginning, rule-based and statistical DDoS detection approaches dominated this field. Such methods can hardly deal with sophisticated attacks, however. As machine learning algorithms evolve and mature, many researchers begin to harness such techniques on big data in detecting and classifying DDoS attacks. For instance, Suresh et al. [26] evaluated a variety of machine learning algorithms in detecting DDoS, including SVM, Naive Bayes, K-means, etc.; Yuan et al. [29] trained a recurrent deep neural network to discover DDoS activities. The results of such methods demonstrate their strong ability in extracting useful knowledge from massive training data to identify DDoS attacks.

However, the negative aspects of learning-based approaches are also apparent. Firstly, most of the learning-based approaches are inexplicable when making predictions. This black-box feature is troublesome because the unexplainable results are difficult for network administrators to review and verify, which could cause potential collateral damage when filtering DDoS traffic. Moreover, learning-based methods are not easily adaptable. The performance of such methods highly depends on the coverage and applicability of the training data, whereas DDoS attacks are diverse and highly dependent on the network environment. A confirmed DDoS attack in one environment may be considered as legitimate in another. Hence, it is difficult for almost all the learning-based approaches to convert a trained DDoS detection model to fit a new network environment.

To address these missing gaps, we design an explainable and adaptable DDoS traffic detection and classification method based on machine learning. It inputs flow-level network traffic and identifies DDoS attackers in two phases: *detection phase* and *classification phase*. In the detection phase, it employs the modified k-nearest neighbors (KNN) algorithm and a k-dimensional tree (KD tree) to detect DDoS attacks with the overall traffic profile. Here, the KD tree can significantly improve detection efficiency and accelerate the query process of KNN. Moreover, we convert the searching space of the KNN model into a semi-decision tree that can reduce the time complexity of traffic monitoring to $O(d)$ in most cases (d is the depth of the semi-decision tree). Once a DDoS threat is detected, our approach enters the classification phase to classify traffic. It will sort the traffic sources based on risk degrees to reduce the collateral damage, then iteratively identify the malicious IP addresses until the traffic profile returns to a benign position in the KNN searching space.

Our approach offers interpretability and adaptability. During a DDoS attack, our approach not only outputs an alert message but also exports a *risk profile* to explain and quantify the attack. The risk profile is the shortest geometrical distance from the current traffic profile to a benign area in the KNN searching space, which provides the network administrators with an explainable summary about the current attack. Besides, users do not need to retrain the detection model to fit it with a new network environment. Our approach allows direct modifications on the KNN searching space and enables users to leverage a variety of prior knowledge to evolve the detection model.

We evaluated our approach in both simulated environments and the real world. We first trained and evaluated our detection model with representative DDoS datasets from public repositories in our simulation environment. The results indicate that the detection model can achieve an accuracy of 0.984 and a recall score of 0.985 when identifying popular DDoS attacks and classifying DDoS traffic, where the model also comes with explainable information to indicate the intensity and category of the attack. Furthermore, as this model is easily adaptable to a new environment, we then transferred the model (with merely some measurement data as input) to a real-world environment that consists of a 50 Gbps link in an ISP-level network. We successfully detected five real-world DDoS attacks from April to May 2020, which we verified with the ISP. The latency of our detection model is also low, even with huge amounts of throughput; with an throughput of 50 Gbps, for example, our approach can complete the detection in around five seconds.

The rest of this paper is organized as follows. After introducing the related works in Sect. 2, we describe the method design in Sect. 3, evaluate our approach in Sect. 4, and conclude this paper in Sect. 6. Of a particular note here is that this paper is an extended version of work published in [14].

2 Related Work

In this section, we present some representative DDoS attack detection and classification methods. According to their basic detection principles, we classify these existing methods as statistical approaches, rule-based approaches, and learning-based approaches.

2.1 Statistical Approaches

Statistical approaches detect DDoS attacks by exploiting statistical properties of benign or malicious network traffic. Generally, these approaches build a statistical model of normal or malicious traffic and then apply a statistical inference test to determine if a new instance follows the model [10]. For example, D-WARD [22] uses a predefined statistical model for legitimate traffic to detect anomalies in the bidirectional traffic statistics for each destination with periodic deviation analysis. Chen [11] proposed a DDoS detection method based on the two-sample t-test, which indicates that the SYN arrival rate of legitimate traffic follows the normal distribution and identifies a DDoS attack by testing the distribution compliance. Zhang et al. [31] proposed a detection method by applying the Auto Regressive Integrated Moving Average model on the available service rate of a protected server. A major drawback of statistical approaches is that as DDoS attacks evolve, DDoS traffic does not always show statistical significance in various aspects. Thus, statistical DDoS detection approaches may be inadequate for identifying modern DDoS attacks.

2.2   Rule-Based Approaches

Rule-based approaches formulate noticeable characteristics of known DDoS attacks and detect actual occurrences of such attacks based on those formulated characteristics. NetBouncer [27] detects illegitimate clients by conducting a set of legitimacy tests of the clients; If a client fails to pass these tests, it will be considered as malicious traffic sources until a particular legitimacy window expires. Wang et al. [28] detects DDoS with an augmented attack tree (AAT), which captures incidents triggered by DDoS traffic and the corresponding state transitions from the view of network traffic transmissions. Limwiwatkul et al. [20] detects ICMP, TCP and UDP flooding attacks by analyzing the packet headers with well-defined rules and conditions. However, it is difficult for all the rule-based approaches to detect unseen attacks. People have to summarize and formulate the features of all the possible DDoS attacks that could happen in the network environment before using such methods, which is hard to achieve in real scenarios.

2.3   Learning-Based Approaches

Over the past few years, more and more researchers began to leverage machine learning to model and detect DDoS attacks [8,13,15,17,18,21,25,30]. Some of these methods utilize unsupervised learning algorithms [9,19,32]. They do not require training before the detection but are sensitive to the selected features and the background traffic. On the other hand, the majority of the methods using supervised learning algorithms cannot provide the users with explainable detection results. Since the dominant machine learning algorithms such as linear regression, multilayer perceptron, and convolutional neural network are similar to black boxes, network administrators need to turn to the raw traffic to dig out information for reviewing the detection results before mitigating the attacks. Thus, although learning-based approaches are usually accurate in detecting DDoS attacks, they are not very reliable in real deployments. Besides, the applicability of these machine learning algorithms highly depends on the training data and environment. It is difficult to quickly transfer a detection model trained in one network environment to another network environment. Different from these previous learning-based approaches, Our approach focuses on the explainability and adaptability of the detection model.

3   Design

Our approach offers DDoS detection and classification at the victim end on a router that sees all the traffic toward and from the victim. Figure 1 illustrates its operational model. It inputs flow-level traffic data from the router that runs widely used traffic capture engines, such as NetFlow [12] and sFlow [24], and monitors the traffic for DDoS detection and classification.

Our approach works in two phases: detection phase and classification phase. It first detects whether there is a DDoS attack or not in the network during

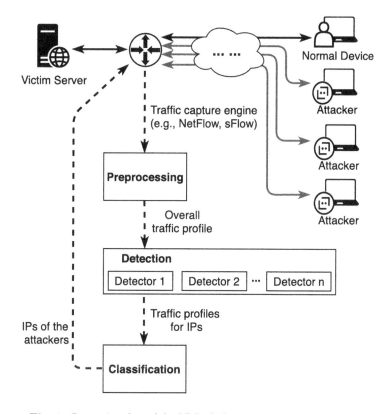

Fig. 1. Operational model of DDoS detection and classification.

the detection phase. To provide a comprehensive protection to the victim, our approach can employ multiple detectors, with each focusing on certain types of DDoS attacks. Once a DDoS attack is detected, it then enters the classification phase. It generates a traffic profile p for every individual IP address, classifies traffic at a fine granularity according to IP traffic profiles, and outputs malicious IP addresses for further actions.

Our approach monitors the traffic in batches. Each batch is a uniform time bin, t, which is also the most basic detection unit. In our implementation, we set each batch as 5 s. During each batch t, the preprocessing module of our approach extracts from the input data features to form different types of overall traffic profiles. A profile can be denoted as S, with $S = \{f_1, f_2, f_3, ..., f_n\}$, where f_n denotes the value of the n-th feature during batch t. The features in S depend on the detectors we use, as each detector may need a different traffic profile with different features.

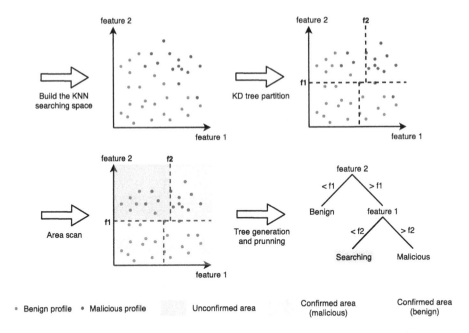

Fig. 2. A DDoS detector with the modified KNN algorithm and KD tree.

3.1   Detection Phase

The goal of the detection phase is to determine whether a DDoS attack is present or not according to the current traffic profile S. We use the KNN algorithm to achieve this. The KNN algorithm is a non-parametric method used for classification, which finds the k nearest neighbors of the traffic profile S and use their classifications to vote for the label of S. This algorithm is simple, straightforward, and reliable. Users can also choose to build multiple KNN detection models to detect a variety of DDoS attacks, as Fig. 1 shows.

In our implementation, we constructed five detection models. For example, we chose six features to construct the traffic profile for the TCP SYN flood detection model, which are the number of TCP bytes, the number of TCP packets, the ratio of inbound TCP packet number to outbound TCP packet number, the number of SYN flags, the number of flows, and the number of PSH flags.

The reason for building multiple KNN models to tackle different attacks instead of building one complicated KNN model is to avoid the curse of dimensionality [16]. A detection model that can tackle different types of attacks usually needs to process data in high-dimensional spaces. However, the increase in the number of dimensions of a dataset can make the searching space sparser. We thus need much more training data to cover the searching space; otherwise the accuracy of the detection model would be unsatisfactory. As a solution to this problem, we construct multiple KNN models to cover different attacks, with each having only a few features.

The KNN algorithm has one weakness, however. Although it takes little time to train the model, the prediction requires a time complexity of $O(nlogn)$ to complete because it needs to enumerate the data points in the searching space to find k nearest neighbors. Hence, we leverage the KD tree to partition the searching space, thus reducing the number of data points to enumerate. With the KD tree, whenever there is an incoming profile, we only need to search a sub-area to predict the result. Figure 2 shows a simple example where only two features are included in the training and prediction.

Furthermore, according to our experimental results, compared with legitimate traffic profiles, most DDoS profiles have relatively big differences. This leads to an interesting fact that most of the searching areas partitioned by the KD tree only have either benign traffic profiles or malicious traffic profiles. As shown by the red and green areas in Fig. 2, we define the searching area as a confirmed area if one type of the traffic profiles dominate the area and the number of any other type of traffic profiles is smaller than $k/2$. If the current traffic profile S falls within a confirmed area, we can directly label the profile S with the identity of the confirmed area without conducting any KNN queries. Thus, we convert the original KNN query process into a tree-like data structure. The detection module will only trigger the search of nearest neighbors when the traffic profile S falls within an unconfirmed area. If DDoS attacks do not happen frequently, this tree-like data structure can reduce the time complexity for traffic monitoring to $O(d)$, where d is the depth of the tree.

Explainability: Once an anomaly is detected, our approach not only outputs an alert message but also exports a value to explain and quantify the anomaly. Such value is the risk profile Δ ($\Delta = (m, \delta)$), which provides the network administrators with an explainable summary about the current attack. Here, m is the name of the feature in the traffic profile S that causes the anomaly. This attribute helps the network administrator determine the attack status and pinpoint the root cause. δ is the value by which feature f_m needs to be reduced to make the traffic profile S return back to a benign space. In other words, δ is the shortest distance from the current traffic profile to a legitimate traffic profile in the KNN searching space.

To figure out m and calculate δ, we need to calculate the average traffic profile $\overline{p}$ for each distinct IP address first, where $\overline{p} = S/number\_of\_ips$. Then, we use Eq. 1 to calculate δ.

$$S_\Delta = S - L$$

$$\delta = max(\frac{f_1^{(S_\Delta)}}{f_1^{(\overline{p})}}, \frac{f_2^{(S_\Delta)}}{f_2^{(\overline{p})}}, \frac{f_3^{(S_\Delta)}}{f_3^{(\overline{p})}}, ..., \frac{f_n^{(S_\Delta)}}{f_n^{(\overline{p})}}) \quad (1)$$

Here, L is the closest traffic profile in a benign space, which can be found with the breadth-first search on the semi-decision tree; $f_n^{(S)}$ denotes the n-th feature in profile S.

In a few cases, there can be more than one shortest distance, which means $\Delta = \{(m_1, \delta_1), (m_2, \delta_2), ..., (m_n, \delta_n)\}$. We consider the anomalies are caused by legitimate flash crowds under these circumstances, since the overall traffic is still in a reasonable shape. Hence, there could be a large surge of legitimate traffic focusing on specific hosts in the network and the detection program will turn over decisions to the network administrator for next measures.

3.2   Phase Two: Classification

The objective of the classification phase is to recognize the malicious IP addresses and output them for DDoS traffic filtering. Of a particular note is that the classification module will only be activated after some anomalies have been detected in the detection phase.

The design philosophy of the traffic classification is that the traffic profile S is currently in a malicious position, and we need to restrict the traffic from the most suspicious IP addresses so that the traffic profile can return to a benign area.

We conduct the classification for malicious sources by building a traffic profile p for each IP address. The profile p should have the same attributes as the overall traffic profile S. The only difference is that the values of features in p are calculated from the traffic of each individual IP, while the values of features in S are calculated from the overall traffic in the network. Afterwards, we sort the IP addresses in the decreasing order of the risk degree, where the risk degree is a number indicates how suspicious an IP is. According to the risk profile Δ ($\Delta = (m, \delta)$) we obtained from the DDoS detection phase, we define the risk degree of an IP address as $f_m^{(p)}$. Finally, we conduct traffic filtering on IP addresses in such an order until the overall traffic profile returns to a benign area.

However, because legitimate clients sometimes may have significant risk degrees as well. Classifying the IP addresses only according to the risk degree may cause significant collateral damage. To address this issue, we also need to minimize the impact on other features of the overall traffic profile S when determining the malicious traffic sources. We consider this as an optimization problem with two constraints, which can be demonstrated as Eq. 2. Here, G denotes the complete set of IP addresses we have seen during the DDoS attack, G_m denotes the set of malicious IP addresses that the classification program will output, and $p^{(i)}$ denotes the traffic profile of the ith-IP.

$$
\begin{aligned}
\operatorname*{argmax}_{G_m} f(G, G_m) &= \sum_{g \in G, g \notin G_m} \sum_{i \in g} \left\| p^{(i)} \right\|_2 \\
&= \sum_{g \in G, g \notin G_m} \sum_{i \in g} \sqrt{\sum_{k=1}^{n} \left| f_k^{p^{(i)}} \right|^2},
\end{aligned}
\tag{2}
$$

$$
\text{subject to: } \sum_{g \in G_m} \sum_{i \in g} p_m^i \geq \delta,
\tag{3}
$$

$$
G_m \subseteq G.
$$

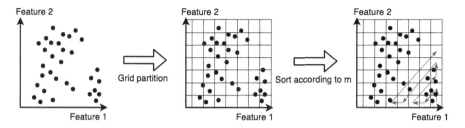

Fig. 3. An example of the classification process, where the dots in the coordinate system are traffic profiles for IP addresses and m is Feature 1.

Equation 3 shows two constraints: (1) after eliminating all the traffic from malicious IP addresses, set G_m, the overall traffic profile should return to a benign area; (2) the malicious IP set G_m should be the subset of the complete IP set G.

Algorithm 1. Recognition of malicious IPs with grid sorting

1: **Input:** risk profile $\Delta = (m, \delta)$
2: **Input:** Complete IP set G
3: Initialize set G_m to store the malicious IP addresses
4: Grid partitioning: $G = \{g_1, g_2, g_3, ..., g_n\}$
5: $G.sort()$ ▷ in decreasing order of feature m and increasing order of other features
6: **for** g in G **do**
7:    $G\_m.add(g.items())$
8:    $val \longleftarrow \sum_{i \in g} f_m^{p^{(i)}}$
9:    $total\_eliminated \longleftarrow val + total\_eliminated$
10:    **if** $total\_eliminated >= \delta$ **then**
11:       **Return** G_m
12:    **end if**
13: **end for**

Deriving the optimal solution of this optimization problem is expensive, especially when the network we are monitoring is at the ISP-level. Hence, we designed Algorithm 1 to get the near-optimal solution G_m efficiently. Since the time complexity of sorting the IPs according to the risk degree is $O(nlogn)$, the algorithm conducts the grid partitioning on the searching space to accelerate the IP classification. Then, we need to eliminate IP addresses along the m axis and minimize impacts on other features at the same time. With this grid configuration, we can always find a corner grid g_m that has the largest value on feature m but also has the smallest values on irrelevant features. The classifier considers the grid g_m as the most suspicious grid and gives it the highest priority in classification. Afterwards, the algorithm sorts the remaining grids in the decreasing order of feature m and increasing order of other features. Finally, the algorithm eliminates the IPs with the unit of a grid in such order until the overall traffic profile return to the benign area. Figure 3 shows an example of such procedure.

3.3   Adaptability

The proposed method features good adaptability, which means the users do not need to retrain the proposed model to fit it into a new network environment. We can use a variety of prior knowledge to evolve the model, making it even robust to the different environments.

Here, we assume the user will have some types of limited information about the new network environment as prior knowledge. Such information includes the measurement data or link bandwidth information about the network environment, some training samples for online learning, and the incomplete threshold values for DDoS detection. Any type of the above information can evolve the detection model and help the model adapt to the new environment.

Network Traffic Measurement. Assuming that we have the measurement data about the new network environment, we can normalize the KNN searching space from the trained environment to the new environment according to the traffic distributions of the two networks. The easiest way is using min-max normalization for the converting.

$$l = max(D_{new}[:, i]) - min(D_{new}[:, i])$$
$$\widehat{D}[:, i] = l \cdot \frac{D[:, i] - min(D[:, i])}{max(D[:, i]) - min(D[:, i])} \tag{4}$$

Equation 4 shows the converting procedure, where D denotes the original training dataset and D_{new} denotes the sampled traffic from the new network environment. By mapping the original training data to the new network environment, our approach is able to conduct DDoS detection without retraining nor re-collecting the training data.

Online Learning. If the traffic monitoring system can obtain labeled traffic with the system running, we can conduct online learning on the proposed detection model, thus making it gradually fit a new environment. The KNN algorithm does not require training, making it very suitable and efficient to conduct online learning. However, the KD-tree, along with the confirmed areas, needs to refresh to reflect new knowledge. We can control the program to update the classifier only during the idle time to reduce the performance impact on the detection system. Nevertheless, the time complexity of refreshing the model is only O(n).

Incomplete Thresholds. In some circumstances, users may know some incomplete threshold values or detection rules in a new network environment. They can then use the preliminary knowledge to build a decision tree and merge it with the trained classifier, a tree-like data structure. If the prior knowledge of the new environment contradicts with the trained detection model, the user can manually indicate the decision priority.

4   Evaluation

After implementing our approach, we trained the detection model with existing DDoS datasets and tested our approach in both simulation and real network environments to evaluate its performance. We also utilized FastNetMon [23], a commercial DDoS detection program, to conduct comparison tests with our approach. FastNetMon is a threshold-based DDoS detection program widely used in middle and small-sized enterprises due to its high efficiency and accuracy. Overall, the evaluation results show that our approach can accurately detect DDoS threats with a relatively low latency. Moreover, according to the result of real-world deployment, our approach can easily fit a new network environment without retraining.

4.1   Model Training

Table 1. Datasets for training and testing.

Dataset name	Format	Attack type
DRAPA 2009 DDoS [3]	pcap	TCP SYN flood attack
CAIDA 2007 DDoS [2]	pcap	ICMP flood attack
FRGP NTP Flow Data [5]	Argus flows	NTP reflection attack
DDoS Chargen 2016 [6]	Flow-tools	UDP reflection and amplification attacks

We picked some representative DDoS datasets from public repositories to train and test our approach. Table 1 shows the datasets we used and the types of attacks they contain. Those datasets can cover at least five types of DDoS attacks, which are TCP SYN flood attacks, ICMP flood attacks, UDP flood attacks, NTP reflection attacks, and UDP reflection and amplification attacks based on Chargen protocol. Thus, we trained five DDoS detection models respectively from the datasets. These models can collaborate to provide protections to the victim server.

The training datasets are in different formats, ranges from fine-grained pcap format to flow-level descriptions of the connections. Our approach works above the flow-level. Thus, to preprocess the data, we converted the original datasets to traffic profiles according to different detection models with the granularity of five seconds. We also sampled a small portion (around 10%) of data from the DDoS datasets as the testing datasets. Those selected datasets would not participate in the model training, but would appear in the testing phase.

As Table 2 shows, we selected five sets of features to train five different detectors. These detectors aimed at TCP SYN flood, ICMP flood, NTP reflection attack, UDP reflection attack, and UDP amplification attack, respectively. The most frequently used feature was the ratio of the inbound traffic volume to the outbound traffic volume. We found this feature plays an important role

Table 2. Features we use for detecting and classifying different categories of DDoS attacks.

Attack type	Features we use
TCP SYN flood attack	#inbound TCP packets/#outbound TCP packets, #TCP bytes, #TCP packets, #SYN flags, #flows, #PSH flags
ICMP flood attack	#inbound ICMP packets/#outbound ICMP packets, #ICMP bytes, #ICMP packets, #echo requests, #echo replies
NTP reflection attack	#inbound NTP packets/#outbound NTP packets, #inbound NTP bytes/#outbound NTP bytes, #NTP bytes, #NTP packets
UDP reflection attack	#inbound UDP bytes/#outbound UDP bytes, #inbound UDP packets/#outbound UDP packets, #UDP bytes, #UDP packets
UDP amplification attack	#inbound UDP packets/#outbound UDP packets, #UDP packets, #UDP bytes

in identifying the majority of DDoS attacks. Other than this, each attack has some specific features that are particularly useful for detection. For example, the number of NTP bytes and the number of NTP packets are essential to detect NTP reflection attacks, but not useful at all for detecting TCP SYN flood attacks.

4.2 Evaluation Under Simulation Environment

We first built a simulation environment to get convenient and efficient tests on the proposed method. To simulate the legitimate background traffic, we sampled network traffic from one router of the Front Range GigaPop (FRGP) [1], a well-known regional Internet service provider (ISP). During the evaluation, we converted the background traffic to traffic profiles and kept replaying them to the detection model. Simultaneously, we replayed the DDoS attack traffic, fine-tuning the traffic volume from a small size to an overwhelming size for mimicking the real scenario.

Figure 4 shows the performance of the DDoS threat detection. The proposed approach surpasses FastNetMon in both the accuracy score and recall score, which means it performs better at identifying DDoS threats. However, our approach is slightly inferior to FastNetMon at the precision score and false positive rate, which means our approach is more likely to label legitimate traffic as malicious. Fortunately, the explicable detection results can help network administrators to exclude false positive alarms quickly.

As for the traffic classification, we conducted access control on the malicious IP addresses reported by our approach and FastNetMon in the simulation environment, and then measured the network situation. Figure 5 shows the

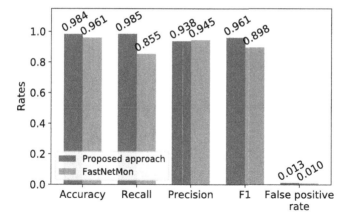

Fig. 4. Detection accuracy.

measurement results, where the y-axis indicates the number of packets. By mitigating all the traffic from the attackers classified by the two programs, we can see our approach can eliminate more malicious traffic than FastNetMon. The only drawback of our approach is that the classification will only be triggered when an attack is detected. Once the traffic profile returns to a legitimate area, our approach would not keep classifying malicious IP addresses until the overall traffic profile turns to hazardous again. Thus, there are periodic fluctuations on the number of packets for our approach in the figure.

4.3 Real-World Deployment

In addition to the evaluation under emulation environments, we deployed over approach on a 50 Gbps link in FRGP to test whether it can capture any DDoS traces in real world and evaluate its adaptability. We measured the network environment in the FRGP link and conducted profile normalization to map the training data to the new environment. We also used a newly developed flow-capture tool named FlowRide to keep streaming flow-level information to our approach every five seconds. A preprocessing program converts the flow records into the overall traffic profiles and IP-level traffic profiles. Each IP traffic profile is indexed by the feature numbers for prompt queries.

We deployed our DDoS detection approach from April 20th, 2020 to May 20th, 2020. During this period, the proposed approach detected six DDoS attacks. After manually verifying, five of the detection results are confirmed to be true positives, which contains two NTP attacks, a TCP SYN flood attack, a DNS reflection attack, and a bandwidth exhausting attack. The only fly in the ointment is that we missed a SYNACK DrDoS attack in the end of April. However, this attack is very rare and targeted the stateful firewall in front of a large AS. The training data did not contain the characteristics of the attack, making our approach difficult to capture it.

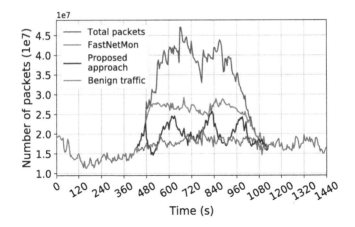

Fig. 5. Performance of traffic classification.

The real-world deployment also provides a good opportunity to test the delay with large throughput. We deployed our program on an Intel Xeon Silver 4116 processor with a RAM of 64 GB. Then, we measured the delay time of our approach and present the result in Fig. 6. From the figure we can see that the delay time is very short when there are no attacks happening. The detection model is similar to a decision tree and it will directly output the results without conducting any KNN queries if the traffic profile is in a good shape. Thus, the majority of time is spent on the data preprocessing when monitoring the traffic. When there is considerable DDoS attack traffic coming in, the delay time begins to increase. However, the detection and classification time is still less than the preprocessing time, costing merely two seconds for each. Besides, the total delay time does not increase significantly with the increase of the number of detection models. This is because only one model will be busy conducting queries at one time in typical cases. In conclusion, our approach is efficient when detecting and classifying DDoS traffic. With delays of around two seconds during idle time and six seconds during DDoS peak, our approach is able to give timely protections to the victim server.

5   Discussions

A primary contribution of this approach is to offer a learning-based DDoS detection solution that features good explainability and adaptability. However, this approach has the following limitations:

- As a learning-based approach, our method may not able to tackle zero-day DDoS attacks. Although the training data can be enhanced to cover more types of DDoS attacks to improve the capability of our approach, nonetheless, if the training does not include particular DDoS traffic, this approach probably will not be able to detect them.

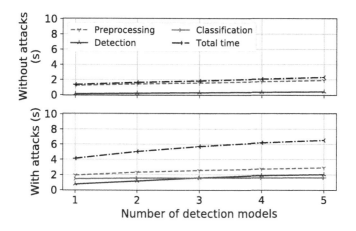

Fig. 6. Delay time (deployed on a 50 Gbps link).

– Due to the characteristic of KNN algorithm, our approach may be vulnerable to adversarial attacks. We can utilize some adversarial machine learning techniques such as data smoothing to fix this problem, but it will inevitably decrease the detection accuracy.

In addition, our approach faces several open issues as possible future working items:

– We can leverage some other explainable machine learning algorithms such as random forests to enhance our approach. Furthermore, it is meaningful to compare the current algorithm with random forests.
– More features may be explored to improve the accuracy for detecting certain complicated DDoS attacks.
– We can further enhance the evaluation of this work by testing the efficacy of our traffic classification algorithm.

6   Conclusions

This paper proposes a learning-based approach to detecting and classifying DDoS traffic. Compared with the existing approaches, the proposed method offers (1) explainability and (2) adaptability. With the KD tree and the modified KNN algorithm, this approach generates a tree-like classifier, which not only makes predictions fast but also provides the network administrator with a clear perspective of the network conditions. Furthermore, people can easily adapt the detection model to a different environment by using various prior knowledge *without* retraining the model from scratch. Benefiting from the grid sorting, the classification module can reduce collateral damage to the maximum extent and generate the results promptly.

We trained the detection model with representative DDoS datasets from public repositories in our simulation environment. We then evaluated this approach in both simulated environments and a real setting. The evaluation results show the efficacy and efficiency of this approach in both settings, as well as its adaptability from the small simulated environments to a real ISP setting. In addition, this approach comes with explainable information to indicate the intensity and category of the attack.

Acknowledgments. This project is the result of funding provided by the Science and Technology Directorate of the United States Department of Homeland Security under contract number D15PC00204. The views and conclusions contained herein are those of the authors and should not be interpreted necessarily representing the official policies or endorsements, either expressed or implied, of the Department of Homeland Security or the US Government.

References

1. Introduction of the front range GigaPOP (FRGP). https://www.frgp.net/intro.shtml
2. The CAIDA UCSD "DDoS attack 2007" dataset (2007). https://www.caida.org/data/passive/ddos-20070804_dataset.xml. CAIDA
3. DARPA 2009 intrusion detection dataset (Colorado State University) (2009). http://www.darpa2009.netsec.colostate.edu/
4. National cyber awareness system: Security tip - understanding Denial-of-Service Attacks (2009). https://www.us-cert.gov/ncas/tips/ST04-015. US-Cert
5. FRGP NTP flow data - NTP reflection attack (2014). https://www.impactcybertrust.org/dataset_view?idDataset=776. University of Southern California-Information Sciences Institute
6. DDoS Chargen 2016 dataset - Internet traffic data containing a DDoS attack based on UDP Chargen protocol (2016). https://www.impactcybertrust.org/dataset_view?idDataset=693. Merit Network Inc
7. Cisco annual internet report (2018–2023) white paper (2020). https://www.cisco.com/c/en/us/solutions/executive-perspectives/annual-internet-report
8. Barati, M., Abdullah, A., Udzir, N.I., Mahmod, R., Mustapha, N.: Distributed denial of service detection using hybrid machine learning technique. In: International Symposium on Biometrics and Security Technologies, pp. 268–273. IEEE (2014)
9. Bhaya, W., EbadyManaa, M.: DDoS attack detection approach using an efficient cluster analysis in large data scale. In: Annual Conference on New Trends in Information & Communications Technology Applications, pp. 168–173. IEEE (2017)
10. Bhuyan, M.H., Kashyap, H.J., Bhattacharyya, D.K., Kalita, J.K.: Detecting distributed denial of service attacks: methods, tools and future directions. Comput. J. **57**(4), 537–556 (2014)
11. Chen, C.L.: A new detection method for distributed denial-of-service attack traffic based on statistical test. J. Univ. Comput. Sci. **15**(2), 488–504 (2009)
12. Claise, B.: Cisco systems netflow services export version 9. RFC 3954 (2004)
13. Doshi, R., Apthorpe, N., Feamster, N.: Machine learning DDoS detection for consumer Internet of Things devices. In: IEEE Security and Privacy Workshops, pp. 29–35 (2018)
14. Feng, Y., Li, J.: Towards explicable and adaptive DDoS traffic classification. In: The 21st Passive and Active Measurement Conference - Poster, March 2020

15. Feng, Y., Li, J., Nguyen, T.: Application-layer DDoS defense with reinforcement learning. In: IEEE/ACM International Symposium on Quality of Service (2020)
16. Friedman, J.H.: On bias, variance, 0/1-loss, and the curse-of-dimensionality. Data Min. Knowl. Discov. **1**(1), 55–77 (1997). https://doi.org/10.1023/A:1009778005914
17. He, Z., Zhang, T., Lee, R.B.: Machine learning based DDoS attack detection from source side in cloud. In: The 4th International Conference on Cyber Security and Cloud Computing (CSCloud), pp. 114–120 (2017)
18. Kokila, R., Selvi, S.T., Govindarajan, K.: DDoS detection and analysis in SDN-based environment using support vector machine classifier. In: The Sixth International Conference on Advanced Computing, pp. 205–210. IEEE (2014)
19. Lee, K., Kim, J., Kwon, K.H., Han, Y., Kim, S.: DDoS attack detection method using cluster analysis. Expert Syst. Appl. **34**(3), 1659–1665 (2008)
20. Limwiwatkul, L., Rungsawang, A.: Distributed denial of service detection using TCP/IP header and traffic measurement analysis. IEEE International Symposium on Communications and Information Technology, vol. 1, pp. 605–610 (2004)
21. Lu, K., Wu, D., Fan, J., Todorovic, S., Nucci, A.: Robust and efficient detection of DDoS attacks for large-scale internet. Comput. Netw. **51**(18), 5036–5056 (2007)
22. Mirkovic, J., Reiher, P.: D-WARD: a source-end defense against flooding denial-of-service attacks. IEEE Trans. Dependable Secure Comput. **2**(3), 216–232 (2005)
23. Odintsov, P.: FastNetMon-very fast DDoS analyzer with sflow/netflow/mirror support. https://github.com/pavel-odintsov/fastnetmon/
24. Panchen, S., Phaal, P., McKee, N.: InMon corporation's sFlow: a method for monitoring traffic in switched and routed networks (2001)
25. Seo, J., Lee, C., Shon, T., Cho, K.-H., Moon, J.: A new DDoS detection model using multiple SVMs and TRA. In: Enokido, T., Yan, L., Xiao, B., Kim, D., Dai, Y., Yang, L.T. (eds.) EUC 2005. LNCS, vol. 3823, pp. 976–985. Springer, Heidelberg (2005). https://doi.org/10.1007/11596042_100
26. Suresh, M., Anitha, R.: Evaluating machine learning algorithms for detecting DDoS attacks. In: Wyld, D.C., Wozniak, M., Chaki, N., Meghanathan, N., Nagamalai, D. (eds.) CNSA 2011. CCIS, vol. 196, pp. 441–452. Springer, Heidelberg (2011). https://doi.org/10.1007/978-3-642-22540-6_42
27. Thomas, R., Mark, B., Johnson, T., Croall, J.: NetBouncer: client-legitimacy-based high-performance DDoS filtering. In: Proceedings DARPA Information Survivability Conference and Exposition, vol. 1, pp. 14–25. IEEE (2003)
28. Wang, J., Phan, R.C.W., Whitley, J.N., Parish, D.J.: Augmented attack tree modeling of distributed denial of services and tree based attack detection method. In: The 10th IEEE International Conference on Computer and Information Technology, pp. 1009–1014 (2010)
29. Yuan, X., Li, C., Li, X.: DeepDefense: identifying DDoS attack via deep learning. In: IEEE International Conference on Smart Computing, pp. 1–8 (2017)
30. Zekri, M., El Kafhali, S., Aboutabit, N., Saadi, Y.: DDoS attack detection using machine learning techniques in cloud computing environments. In: The 3rd International Conference of Cloud Computing Technologies and Applications, pp. 1–7. IEEE (2017)
31. Zhang, G., Jiang, S., Wei, G., Guan, Q.: A prediction-based detection algorithm against distributed denial-of-service attacks. In: International Conference on Wireless Communications and Mobile Computing: Connecting the World Wirelessly, pp. 106–110 (2009)
32. Zi, L., Yearwood, J., Wu, X.W.: Adaptive clustering with feature ranking for DDoS attacks detection. In: The Fourth International Conference on Network and System Security, pp. 281–286. IEEE (2010)

Forecasting Network Intrusions from Security Logs Using LSTMs

W. Graham Mueller$^{(\boxtimes)}$ ⓘ, Alex Memory ⓘ, and Kyle Bartrem

Leidos, Inc., Arlington, VA 22203, USA
{muellerwg,memoryac,bartremk}@leidos.com

Abstract. Computer network intrusions are of increasing concern to governments, companies, and other institutions. While technologies such as Intrusion Detection Systems (IDS) are growing in sophistication and adoption, early warning of intrusion attempts could help cybersecurity practitioners put defenses in place early and mitigate the effects of cyberattacks. It is widely known that cyberattacks progress through stages, which suggests that forecasting network intrusions may be possible if we are able to identify certain precursors. Despite this potential, forecasting intrusions remains a difficult problem. By leveraging the rapidly growing and widely varying data available from network monitoring and Security Information and Event Management (SIEM) systems, as well as recent advances in deep learning, we introduce a novel intrusion forecasting application. Using six months of data from a real, large organization, we demonstrate that this provides improved intrusion forecasting accuracy compared to existing methods.

Keywords: Network intrusion · Neural networks · Forecasting · Cybersecurity

1 Introduction

Computer network intrusions are of increasing concern to governments, companies, and other institutions. For example, on average the cost of a dynamic denial of service (DDoS) attack on an enterprise is over two million US dollars [8] and information leaks can cost millions to mitigate [17]. While techniques to detect intrusions using *intrusion detection systems* (IDS) are widely used, early warning of intrusion attempts could help network administrators put defenses in place early and mitigate the effects of attacks.

Cyberattacks are well known to progress through stages. For example, according to the Cyber Kill Chain® framework, exploitation attacks follow delivery attacks, which follow reconnaissance attacks [6]. This suggests that networking intrusions could be forecasted if we learn to detect their precursors. With the rapid growth of *network monitoring* and SIEM systems, evidence of those precursors may exist in the form of logged security events. However, detecting precursors of attacks at varying time scales and among the noise present in an

© Springer Nature Switzerland AG 2020
G. Wang et al. (Eds.): MLHat 2020, CCIS 1271, pp. 122–137, 2020.
https://doi.org/10.1007/978-3-030-59621-7_7

operational network has proved difficult. Combined with rich evidence from network security monitor logs in a real SIEM, we apply recent advances in deep learning – specifically, long short-term memory (LSTM) neural networks [5] – and demonstrate improved intrusion forecasting accuracy, compared to earlier methods.

We use a dataset collected from a real, anonymous organization. This dataset includes the number and category of intrusion detection system alerts as well as aggregated network traffic data captured by the organization's SIEM system. Specifically, we use a large number of high level network events captured from a network monitor. We examine the utility of these features for forecasting near-term network intrusions as well as the effect of the length of the forecasting window on forecast accuracy.

Our contributions include a novel application of deep learning to the time series intrusion forecasting problem and also an extensive empirical evaluation of the approach on intrusion in a large scale, real organization. The rest of this paper is organized as follows. In Sect. 2 we describe related work. In Sect. 3, we describe in detail the data we used. In Sect. 4 we define the models we use to forecast intrusion events. In Sect. 5 we present our results from a large empirical evaluation and conclude by suggesting future applications of this work.

2   Related Work

There have been several recent works which have examined forecasting cyberattacks. These works have primarily focused on using past attack data, identifying novel indicators, or a combination of the two to develop forecasting models. For example, Okutan et al. [14] used Auto-Regressive Moving Average to forecast indicators that served as input into a Bayesian Network. Perera et al. [16] analyzed public text using mini-theories to predict attacks. Sarkar et al. [18] examined the utility of using chatter and social relationships on dark web hacker forums as a predictor of future attacks. Goyal et al. [4] used external signals, ARIMAX models, and neural networks to predict cyberattacks at two organizations. Filonov et al. [3] used neural networks to forecast faults in multivariate industrial time series.

The problem of detecting network intrusions has also been studied recently, including work by [9,10,12], and [1]. Each of these studies use publicly available network intrusion datasets including SCX-IDS 2012, CIDDS-001, KDD98, and UNM-lpr. These datasets are not ideal in that they are generated data from a small number of servers and may not reflect modern network systems due to their age. Our data is from a large corporate network and may offer different insights into network intrusion event, although our data lacks ground truth, we use the data generated by network monitoring software as a proxy.

Our earlier work considered alternative approaches such as using causal discovery algorithms to identify causal relationships using SIEM data and open source threat indicators [13] and applying statistical relational learning to fuse cyber attack sensor outputs and generate attack predictions [11].

Many of these works showed promising results and highlighted the difficulty of the forecasting problem. In this vein, Tavabi et al. [20] identified some of the challenges associated with forecasting cyberattacks which make it past an organization's firewall. Okutan et al. [15] identified the potentially non-stationary nature of the relationship between input signals and cyber attack time series.

Our work is a continuation of these research threads and is unique in that the data was aggregated on an hourly, rather than daily, basis. The approach used by Shen et al. is similar to ours, however their work is focused on predicting discrete events, while our work focuses on forecasting aggregate alerts. In addition, we include both network traffic data and suspected network intrusion events. Furthermore, the forecasting utility of many of the network traffic features has not been previously examined. Understanding how predictable individual IDS alerts may also provide insight into the value of these alerts to an organization's Security Operations Center (SOC).

3   Data Description

We use data provided by a large, anonymous organization through query-based access to the organization's SIEM system. We use two primary sources of data:

- Network security logs produced by Zeek[1]
- Network intrusions detected by Suricata[2]

Zeek (previously called BRO) is an open source network security platform that transforms network traffic into high-level event logs. Zeek employs a modular, heuristic-based framework which enables both the collection and analysis of network traffic. Suricata is a signature-based network IDS which also has intrusion prevention (IPS) capabilities. While both technologies collect network traffic and monitor for malicious activity, Suricata is deployed primarily as an alert system whereas Zeek is leveraged for deeper inspection of relevant network traffic.

Both Zeek and Suricata are IDS solutions, though they also play a role in logging and forwarding network traffic to a centralized location such as a SIEM. In a typical corporate network, Zeek and Suricata would be deployed as sensors across each subnet, which would then forward traffic within their respective subnets to the SIEM. This architecture enables cybersecurity practitioners to monitor and analyze traffic across the entire network from one central location. Figure 1 illustrates a simple depiction of this architecture.

From the network security logs extracted from Zeek and Suricata, we extract a set of statistical time series. Each time series has data on an hourly basis and records the count of matching logged events in various categories. Table 1 describes the types of network monitoring data.

We monitored counts of the following types of IDS events: attempted denial of service, attempted information leak, attempted user privilege gain, executable

---

[1] https://zeek.org.

[2] https://suricata-ids.org/.

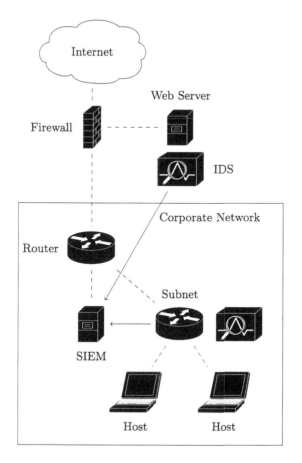

Fig. 1. Network architecture with IDS/SIEM deployment

code was detected, generic protocol command decode, misc. attack, misc. activity, not suspicious traffic, potential corporate privacy violation, potentially bad traffic, detection of a network scan, decode of an RPC query, a suspicious filename was detected, web application attack, access to a potentially vulnerable web application, successful user privilege gain, information leak, successful administrator privilege gain, unknown traffic, detection of a non-standard protocol or event, pending threat assessment exploit, detection of a denial of service attack, and detection of a suspicious string. Each IDS event falls into one of three risk levels: low, intermediate, and critical. We describe each IDS event type in Table 2. In Fig. 2, we plot the total counts of events for each risk level, showing that most IDS events have intermediate risk and IDS events in each risk level have both long- and short-term temporal patterns.

We collected the data over a period of two years from March 2018 through March 2020. We found that, due to changing network monitoring policy changes and gaps in monitor coverage, there are several periods of missing data in the full

Table 1. Types of network monitoring time series used to find precursors of future network intrusions. All are hourly counts.

Time series	Description
Destination ports by source	A single source attempting connections to a broad range of destination ports may be malicious
DNS requests by TLD	Get/Post requests to known-malicious domains may indicate host compromise
Inbound connection ports	Specific ports may be unused or reserved, connection attempts may indicate maliciousness
Internal-internal connection ports	Non-regular lateral (internal) movement may indicate an active breach
MIME file type and direction	Specific MIME types may be associated with potentially malicious files or packages
Outbound connection ports	Outbound (internal) beacons to known-malicious destinations may indicate host compromise
Paired FTP command reply codes	Improperly-formed or incomplete FTP reply codes may indicate suspicious activity
Weird events by source IP (1st byte)	Network activity which does not conform to protocols is logged as 'Weird' events

collection. For this reason, we examine a subset of the data from December 2018 through June 2019, when we have complete records for all data types. Collecting data on an hourly basis resulted in a total of $6,083$ observations for 325 random variables. In Fig. 3, we plot a heat map of a selection of log-transformed network monitoring (MIME, SSL, and Weird) and IDS time series, revealing both short- and long-term variability in both types of signals.

Table 2. Network intrusions time series forecasted using our approach. All are hourly counts.

Time series	Description or example	Risk level
Attempted administrator priv. gain	Windows alert generated by an OS attack	Critical
Attempted denial of service	Attempt to exploit server vulnerability	Intermed
Attempted information leak	Attempted exploitation of non-standard OS vulnerability	Intermed
Attempted user privilege gain	Unauthorized attempt to elevate privileges	Critical
Detection of a network scan	Inbound network scan detected	Low
Decode of an RPC query	RPC packets may encapsulate malicious code and must be decoded/inspected	Intermed

(*continued*)

Table 2. (*continued*)

Time series	Description or example	Risk level
Executable code detected	An x86 shell code signature was detected on the network	Critical
Generic protocol command decode	Subnet mask mismatch between the router and a networked device	Low
Misc. activity	Custom or non-standard rule was triggered	Low
Misc. attack	Attempted exploitation of server vulnerability	Intermed
Network trojan was detected	Malicious software or code detected on the network	Critical
Not suspicious traffic	Traffic detected may be malicious depending on its context	Low
Potential corporate privacy viol.	A violation of corporate policy was detected	Critical
Potentially bad traffic	DNS-spoofing attempt	Intermed
Successful administrator priv. gain	Command shell detection, likely indicating system compromise	Critical
Suspicious string was detected	Suspicious FTP traffic detected	Low
Unknown traffic	An unusual or unexpected event has occurred on the network	Low
Web application attack	Attempted web-based attack	Critical

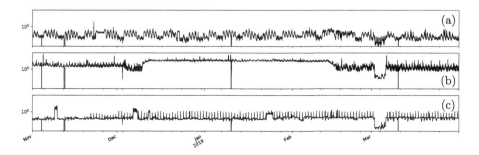

Fig. 2. Totals (log scale) of IDS time series by risk level: (a) critical, (b) intermediate, and (c) low risk.

4   Experimental Setup

The wide variety of signals collected from network monitors is promising as a source of precursors of network intrusion as detected by IDS. Therefore, our goal is to examine whether the security logs collected from network monitors is useful for forecasting the IDS alerts and to determine how much past data, if any, is needed for the forecasting models. In this section, we describe three models for doing this forecasting. For all models, we forecast a length-T time series $y = \{y_1, y_2, \ldots, y_T\}$, producing the approximation $\hat{y}$. For each IDS alert, we develop a forecasting model using the past values of the alert and the past values of the network traffic data (for the LSTM model only). The chosen baseline models help us to determine 1) whether the future values of the IDS alerts are predictable; and 2) whether the past values of the network traffic data are informative to the forecasting models. We perform all experiments on a system with 16 Xeon 2.67GHz cores and 128G of RAM.

4.1   Preprocessing

Machine learning-based forecasting suffers from the curse of dimensionality; we pre-process the data to address issues with dimentionality and to avoid over-fitting. Several of the network monitoring time series are extremely sparse and exhibited little or no variance in the period of interest. To reduce dimensionality and remove irrelevant features, we remove all variables with a variance below one. Eliminating the low-variance variables leaves 113 network traffic variables and 18 IDS alerts. In addition, to avoid overfitting we divided the data into training and validation sets. Additionally, to accommodate differing scales and distributions of the input features, we normalized the individual time series using the mean and standard deviation from the training sets.

4.2   Naïve Baseline

We compare the performance of several forecasting models. The naïve-baseline for non-seasonal data is based on a randomwalk and simply predicts no change in the data.

$$\hat{y}_t = y_{t-1}$$

4.3   ARIMA Baseline

We use a non-seasonal Auto-Regressive Integrated Moving Average (ARIMA) model to forecast the IDS alerts. The full model can be written as

$$y'_t = c + \phi_1 y'_{t-1} + \cdots + \phi_p y'_{t-p} + \theta_1 \epsilon_{t-1} + \ldots \theta_q \epsilon_{t-q} + \epsilon_t$$

where y'_t is a series that has been differenced d times.

We select the parameters p, d, and q for the ARIMA models using the model selection process described by Hyndman and Khandakar [7].

4.4   Long Short-Term Memory

We use a sequence-to-sequence, stacked long short-term memory [5] neural network to forecast the number of IDS alerts. A LSTM cell consists of an input gate, output gate, and a forget gate which control the flow of information through

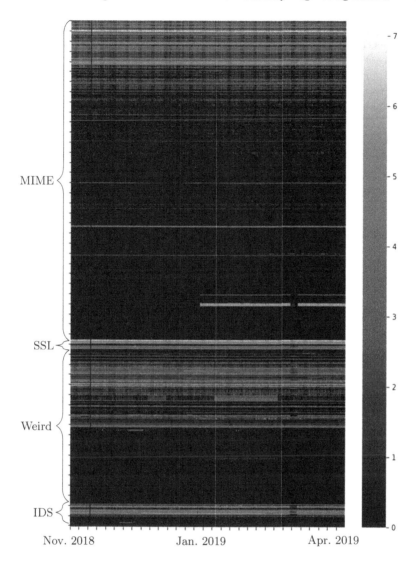

Fig. 3. Heat map (log scale) of time series used in the study.

the unit. LSTMs are trained using backpropagation through time. LSTM is a promising model for intrusion forecasting because long-term dependencies exist between the precursor events recorded by network monitors and the intrusions themselves. For traditional forecasting methods and earlier recurrent neural network architectures, modeling long-term dependencies has been difficult, e.g., due to the vanishing gradient problem [2]. LSTM addresses this problem by carrying outputs across LSTM cells and learning when to forget them.

With the LSTM, we use an additional length-T, multivariate time series of exogenous data $\mathbf{x} = \{\mathbf{x}_1, \ldots, \mathbf{x}_T\}$. Each time step is a length-D vector

$\mathbf{x_t} = \{x_{t,1}, \ldots, x_{t,D}\}$, where dimensionality D is determined by the number of features, 114, which include the network traffic data and the target IDS alert.

Figure 4 illustrates the LSTM architecture we used. The figure shows an unrolled portion of the architecture, where both the recurrence and carry information passed between LSTM cells is shown as arrows from left to right. The input layer is the hourly time series of 114 input features for the historical period $\{\mathbf{x}_{t-H}, \ldots, \mathbf{x}_t\}$ of length H, where we set H equal to a one week period. The first layer of LSTM cells have an output dimensionality of 128, which we chose through empirical experimentation to reflect the complexity of the forecasting task.

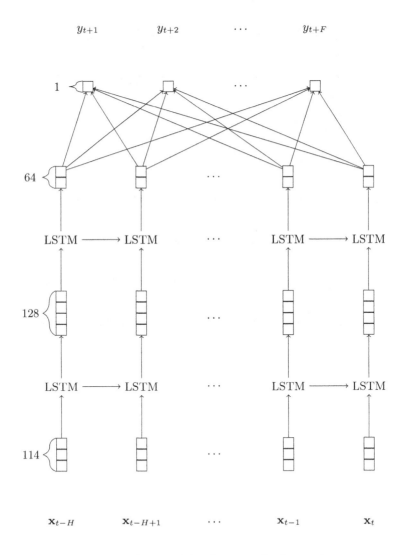

Fig. 4. Unrolled LSTM architecture for forecasting.

The second layer of LSTM cells have an output dimensionality of 64 and use a hyperbolic tangent activation followed by a fully connected layer to the target outputs for the forecast period $\{y_{t+1}, \ldots, y_{t+F}\}$ of length F, where we set the forecast length F equal to a period of 12 h.

To train the neural network, we build 4,090 training examples by varying t hour-by-hour in the training period. We learn weights using stochastic gradient descent with batch sizes of 128 examples each, 20 training epochs, and 200 steps per epoch. Training for each IDS alert category took approximately one hundred minutes.

4.5 Evaluation Criteria

We evaluate each forecast using mean absolute error (MAE). MAE was chosen due to the asymmetric distribution of the underlying time series. For the LSTM models, we created the needed sub-sequences performed batch training with the resulting data. We estimated the parameters for the ARIMA models using all the data in the training set, then computed forecasts for each period in the validation set. In Table 3, we list the MAE for each forecasting method.

5 Results

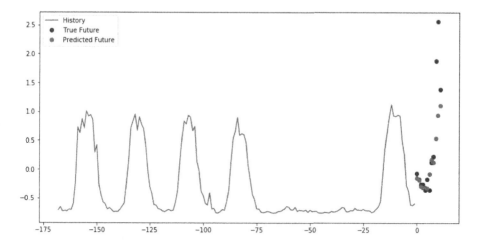

Fig. 5. Example of a forecast for the suspicious string was detected alert

5.1 Detailed Results Analysis

For five of the IDS alerts (see Table 3), the naïve method achieved the smallest MAE. This is due to the low volume of alerts for these categories (see Fig. 6). Each of these alerts exhibited very low volume during the validation period compared to the training period and the variance is driven by rare events.

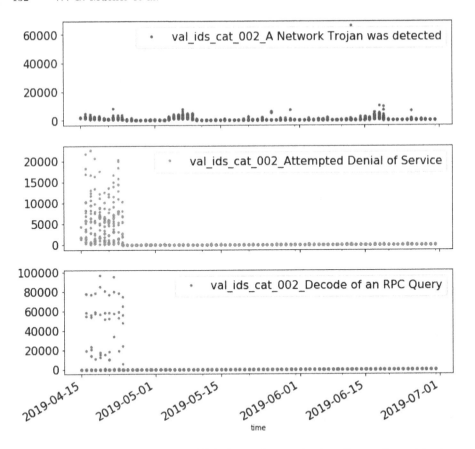

Fig. 6. Examples of low volume IDS alerts where naive baseline performed best

It is also possible that the IDS configurations were changed during the collection period and certain alerts were no longer produced.

ARIMA models achieve the smallest MAE for Attempted Information Leak, Detection of a Network Scan, and Unknown Traffic. This indicates that future values of the IDS alerts were closer to linear functions of the past values, rather than non-linear functions of the past values of network traffic data and IDS alerts.

For several other IDS alerts, the LSTM models are most accurate over the 12-h forecast period. This indicates that the network traffic data captured by the network monitor gives short term indicators of network intrusions. In Fig. 5, we plot the LSTM forecast for Suspicious String Detection, showing the capability of the LSTM forecast to closely match a real, substantial increase in intrusions of that category.

Table 3. Overall results mean absolute error

IDS rule	LSTM	ARIMA	Naïve
A network trojan was detected	0.341	0.068	**0.036**
Attempted admin. priv. gain	1.258	1.409	**1.158**
Attempted denial of service	0.576	0.051	**0.036**
Attempted information leak	0.519	**0.121**	0.228
Attempted user priv. gain	**0.098**	27.2	0.338
Decode of an RPC query	0.332	0.675	**0.039**
Detection of a network scan	1.45	**1.29**	1.80
Executable code was detected	**0.111**	0.253	0.266
Generic protocol command decode	**0.417**	0.311	0.725
Misc activity	**0.196**	2.81	0.259
Misc attack	**0.644**	3.15	0.790
Not suspicious traffic	**0.161**	7.80	0.386
Potential corporate privacy viol.	**0.699**	0.811	1.06
Potentially bad traffic	**0.092**	1.88	0.501
Successful admin. priv. gain	**0.001**	0.062	0.407
Suspicious string was detected	**0.360**	0.143	0.562
Unknown traffic	0.179	**0.099**	0.177
Web application attack	0.360	2.33	**0.133**

5.2   Feature Importance for LSTM Models

For the IDS alerts that the network traffic features showed useful, we consider which features are the most important for forecasting. A common approach to interpreting functions learned by a deep neural networks is to examine the gradients of the output values with respect to input values. For image classification, this technique is known as a saliency map and described by Simonyan et al. [19]. The same technique may be applied to LSTM networks to identify which input series and time lags have the largest influence on the output values (forecasts). This should indicate how output values change with respect to a small change in past values of the input time series. Positive values in the gradients tell us that a small change to that lagged time series value will increase the output value. In order to determine the most impactful network traffic data on each IDS alert, we took a random sample of 500 input sequences and computed the gradients for each sequence with respect of the output.

These gradients reveal a few interesting patterns that hold for many of the IDS alerts. For example, Fig. 7 shows a sample of the gradient values for each input series (unlabeled y-axis) and the time lag on the x-axis. The gradient values quickly vanish beyond the near past. This pattern holds to a varying degree for each of the IDS alerts, indicating only the very recent past is useful for forecasting. Another interesting pattern is the temporal clustering of gradient values exhibited in Fig. 8. This may indicate the LSTM learns some aggregate threshold where changes of the level of any one of the input series lead to changes in the level of IDS alerts.

In order to identify the input series with the greatest impact on the IDS alerts, we average the gradients across time, resulting in ranked list of input series for each LSTM model. Table 4 lists the two input variables with largest average gradient absolute values for the first time step of the forecast. For several of the IDS alerts, the past values of the alert itself are the most important for the forecast. Interestingly, for each of these IDS alerts, ARIMA models performed very poorly, likely due to non-linearity.

For the Potential Corporate Privacy alert, outbound x-mp4a-latm mime type was the most important feature followed by inbound chrome-ext. These mime types are associated with audio files and Google Chrome extensions. Many corporations restrict the use of unauthorized Chrome extensions on their endpoints to reduce the risk of unauthorized access.

Lateral movement is common technique used to gain access to servers and is often achieved through the abuse of ssh public keys, such as those stored in the known hosts folder. The inbound x-pem refers to inbound pem files, a format RSA public keys are often stored as. Unknown pem files might trigger the Attempted User Privilege Gain alert which may explain the importance of this mime type on these forecasting alerts.

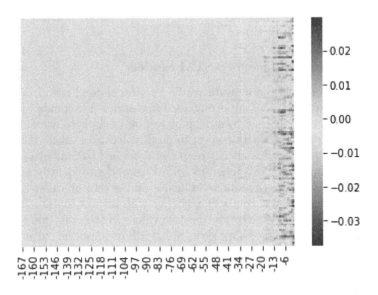

Fig. 7. Example gradients by time lag and input series

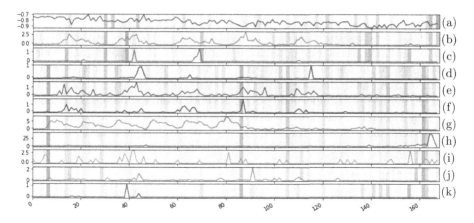

Fig. 8. Feature importance analysis, showing gradients of the predictive intrusion model with respect to input time series: (a) miscellaneous attacks, (b) inbound office documents, (c) outbound RPM operating system packages, (d) inbound remote procedure calls, (e) inbound TIFF images, (f) inbound JPEG images, (g) outbound MP4 audio, (h) outbound RTF text, (i) inbound PGP encryption, (j) outbound Java archives, (k) inbound geospatial map tile data. The gradients are shown as colors overlaid on the time series. Positive gradients are red and negative gradients are blue.

Table 4. Top two features (absolute value of gradient) ranked by the average absolute value of the gradient per IDS alert

IDS	Top two features
Attempted user privilege gain	Attempted User Privilege Gain, application/x-pem:inbound
Executable code	vnd.google-earth.kml+xml:inbound, image/jp2:inbound
Generic protocol	audio/x-mp4a-latm:outbound, application/chrome-ext:inbound
Misc activity	audio/x-mp4a-latm:outbound, text/rss:inbound
Misc attack	Misc Attack, application/soap+xml:inbound
Not suspicious traffic	Not Suspicious Traffic, message/rfc822:outbound
Potential corporate privacy violation	audio/x-mp4a-latm:outbound, application/chrome-ext:inbound
Potentially bad traffic	Potentially Bad Traffic, text/html:inbound
Successful administrator privilege gain	application/soap+xml:inbound, application/msword:outbound

5.3   Potential Applications

Given that the forecasting models have shown some ability to predict the near-term level of IDS alerts, one potential application of these models is to monitor network traffic for unusual activity. IDS alerts that are predictable may not be useful for SOC analysts to monitor, unless they show unusual activity. If the observed number of IDS alerts differs significantly from the predicted number, it may indicate unusual network activity. This may help focus the efforts of SOC analysts and allow them to scrutinize a "normal" level alerts vs an unusual level.

6   Conclusion

We have described a novel security dataset, namely aggregated hourly network traffic and IDS alerts from an anonymous organization and compared LSTM to two well-known benchmarks. We find that IDS alerts can be accurately forecasted up to 12 h ahead and for several of the IDS alerts network traffic provides utility to the forecasting models. The models also indicate that only data from the near past is useful for forecasting models supporting previous research which found strong evidence of non-stationary and model drift in times series involving cyber attack data. Examining the gradients of the LSTM network with respect to the input helps reveal the relationships between the high-level network events and IDS alerts and could be included in a forecasting application to help SOC analysts both understand and prioritize alerts for investigation.

Acknowledgments. Development of the datasets described in this paper was part of the ELLIPSE project. Exploiting Leading Indicators Latent Indicators in Predictive Sensor Environments (ELLIPSE) was supported by the Office of the Director of National Intelligence (ODNI) and the Intelligence Advanced Research Projects Activity (IARPA) via the Air Force Research Laboratory (AFRL) contract number FA8750-16-C-0114. The U.S. Government is authorized to reproduce and distribute reprints for Governmental purposes notwithstanding any copyright annotation thereon.

Disclaimer: The views and conclusions contained herein are those of the authors and should not be interpreted as necessarily representing the official policies or endorsements, either expressed or implied, of ODNI, IARPA, AFRL, or the U.S. Government.

References

1. Althubiti, S.A., Jones, E.M., Roy, K.: LSTM for anomaly-based network intrusion detection. In: 2018 28th International Telecommunication Networks and Applications Conference (ITNAC), pp. 1–3. IEEE (2018)
2. Bengio, Y., Frasconi, P., Simard, P.: The problem of learning long-term dependencies in recurrent networks. In: IEEE International Conference on Neural Networks, pp. 1183–1188. IEEE (1993)
3. Filonov, P., Lavrentyev, A., Vorontsov, A.: Multivariate industrial time series with cyber-attack simulation: fault detection using an LSTM-based predictive data model. arXiv preprint arXiv:1612.06676 (2016)

4. Goyal, P., et al.: Discovering signals from web sources to predict cyber attacks. arXiv preprint arXiv:1806.03342 (2018)
5. Hochreiter, S., Schmidhuber, J.: Long short-term memory. Neural Comput. **9**(8), 1735–1780 (1997)
6. Hutchins, E.M., Cloppert, M.J., Amin, R.M.: Intelligence-driven computer network defense informed by analysis of adversary campaigns and intrusion kill chains. In: Leading Issues in Information Warfare & Security Research, vol. 1, no. 1, p. 80 (2011)
7. Hyndman, R., Khandakar, Y.: Automatic time series forecasting: the forecast package for r 7, 2008 (2007). http://www.jstatsoft.org/v27/i03
8. Kaspersky: DDoS Breach Costs Rise to over $2M for Enterprises finds Kaspersky Lab Report — Kaspersky. https://usa.kaspersky.com/about/press-releases/2018_ddos-breach-costs-rise-to-over-2m-for-enterprises-finds-kaspersky-lab-report
9. Khan, M.A., Karim, M., Kim, Y., et al.: A scalable and hybrid intrusion detection system based on the convolutional-LSTM network. Symmetry **11**(4), 583 (2019)
10. Kim, G., Yi, H., Lee, J., Paek, Y., Yoon, S.: LSTM-based system-call language modeling and robust ensemble method for designing host-based intrusion detection systems. arXiv preprint arXiv:1611.01726 (2016)
11. Memory, A., Mueller, W.G.: Sensor fusion and structured prediction for cyber-attack event networks. In: 15th International Workshop on Mining and Learning with Graphs (MLG) (2019)
12. Mirza, A.H., Cosan, S.: Computer network intrusion detection using sequential LSTM neural networks autoencoders. In: 2018 26th Signal Processing and Communications Applications Conference (SIU), pp. 1–4. IEEE (2018)
13. Mueller, W.G., Memory, A., Bartrem, K.: Causal discovery of cyber attack phases. In: 2019 18th IEEE International Conference On Machine Learning And Applications (ICMLA), pp. 1348–1352. IEEE (2019)
14. Okutan, A., Yang, S.J., McConky, K.: Forecasting cyber attacks with imbalanced data sets and different time granularities. arXiv preprint arXiv:1803.09560 (2018)
15. Okutan, A., Yang, S.J., McConky, K., Werner, G.: Capture: cyberattack forecasting using non-stationary features with time lags. In: 2019 IEEE Conference on Communications and Network Security (CNS), pp. 205–213. IEEE (2019)
16. Perera, I., Hwang, J., Bayas, K., Dorr, B., Wilks, Y.: Cyberattack prediction through public text analysis and mini-theories. In: 2018 IEEE International Conference on Big Data (Big Data), pp. 3001–3010. IEEE (2018)
17. Ponemon Institute: 2018 cost of a data breach study: global overview. Technical report, Ponemon Institute LLC (2018)
18. Sarkar, S., Almukaynizi, M., Shakarian, J., Shakarian, P.: Predicting enterprise cyber incidents using social network analysis on dark web hacker forums. In: International Conference on Cyber Conflict (CYCON U.S.), 14-15 November 2018, Cyber Conflict During Competition, pp. 87–102 (2019). The Cyber Defense Review, Special Edition
19. Simonyan, K., Vedaldi, A., Zisserman, A.: Deep inside convolutional networks: visualising image classification models and saliency maps. arXiv preprint arXiv:1312.6034 (2013)
20. Tavabi, N., Abeliuk, A., Mokhberian, N., Abramson, J., Lerman, K.: Challenges in forecasting malicious events from incomplete data. In: Companion Proceedings of the Web Conference 2020, pp. 603–610 (2020)

DAPT 2020 - Constructing a Benchmark Dataset for Advanced Persistent Threats

Sowmya Myneni[1], Ankur Chowdhary[1(✉)], Abdulhakim Sabur[1],
Sailik Sengupta[1], Garima Agrawal[1], Dijiang Huang[1], and Myong Kang[2(✉)]

[1] Arizona State University, Tempe, AZ, USA
{smyneni2,achaud16,asabur,ssengu15,gsindal,dijiang}@asu.edu
[2] US Naval Research Laboratory, Washington, D.C., USA
myong.kang@nrl.navy.mil

Abstract. Machine learning is being embraced by information security researchers and organizations alike for its potential in detecting attacks that an organization faces, specifically attacks that go undetected by traditional signature-based intrusion detection systems. Along with the ability to process large amounts of data, machine learning brings the potential to detect contextual and collective anomalies, an essential attribute of an ideal threat detection system. Datasets play a vital role in developing machine learning models that are capable of detecting complex and sophisticated threats like Advanced Persistent Threats (APT). However, there is currently no APT-dataset that can be used for modeling and detecting APT attacks. Characterized by the sophistication involved and the determined nature of the APT attackers, these threats are not only difficult to detect but also to model. Generic intrusion datasets have three key limitations - (1) They capture attack traffic at the external endpoints, limiting their usefulness in the context of APTs which comprise of attack vectors within the internal network as well (2) The difference between normal and anomalous behavior is quiet distinguishable in these datasets and thus fails to represent the sophisticated attackers' of APT attacks (3) The data imbalance in existing datasets do not reflect the real-world settings rendering themselves as a benchmark for supervised models and falling short of semi-supervised learning. To address these concerns, in this paper, we propose a dataset DAPT 2020 which consists of attacks that are part of Advanced Persistent Threats (APT). These attacks (1) are hard to distinguish from normal traffic flows but investigate the raw feature space and (2) comprise of traffic on both public-to-private interface and the internal (private) network. Due to the existence of severe class imbalance, we benchmark DAPT 2020 dataset on semi-supervised models and show that they perform poorly trying to detect attack traffic in the various stages of an APT.

Keywords: Advanced Persistent Threat · Benchmark dataset · Stacked Autoencoder (SAE) · Long Term Short Memory (LSTM) · Anomaly detection

Sowmya Myneni and Ankur Chowdhary have equally contributed to this work.

G. Wang et al. (Eds.): MLHat 2020, CCIS 1271, pp. 138–163, 2020.
https://doi.org/10.1007/978-3-030-59621-7_8

1   Introduction

Advanced Persistent Threat (APT) [29] is a form of a cybersecurity threat, posed by well-funded organizations, often to gain crucial information from the target organization. APT is defined by a combination of three words, namely (1) *Advanced:* APT attackers are advanced in terms of attack tools expertise, and attack methods. With attack vectors customized to the target, APT attackers organize the attack into multiple stages. (2) *Persistent:* APT attackers are determined to achieve the attack objective. The attack methods involve the use of evasive techniques to elude security agents deployed by the network defender. (3) *Threat:* The threat part of APT comes from the potential loss of sensitive data or mission-critical components. An APT attack usually consists of five main phases, (1) Reconnaissance (2) Foothold Establishment (3) Lateral Movement (4) Data Exfiltration, and (5) Post-Exfiltration [1].

A vast array of research exists in the area of anomaly detection [11], and traditional intrusion detection systems as a means of identification of slow and low attacks such as APT. These encompass methods to detect abnormal behaviors through the use of rule-based engines [15,28,54], machine learning algorithms [18], in general, and more recently, deep learning architectures [53] in particular. These methods focus mostly on detecting anomalies in external traffic packets, i.e., at the interface of the external and internal network. A survey of industry professionals conducted by Trend Micro [34] shows only 25.1% of the participants are familiar with APTs and 53.1% consider that APTs are similar to traditional attack vectors. However, the detection of Advanced Persistent Threat (APT) that involves the identification of long-term attack behavior both over the public and private channels is fundamentally different.

While attackers in the context of APTs leverage tools and techniques similar to those used in the external attack vectors, the mode of operation and the goal of these attacks is different from the traditional single-stage attacks. Traditional intrusion detection techniques such as pattern/signature matching, machine learning, etc. cannot detect APTs effectively because they are often designed to detect individual (known) attack patterns or methods as opposed to a threat that involves several interconnected malicious activities. Furthermore, performance on individual phases of APTs, as we show based on results of semi-supervised machine learning models (used in anomaly detection) is far from being effective (see auc-roc-pr). The *stealthiness, adaptability,* and *persistence* of APTs makes detection and prevention of such threats, by present methods, quite challenging [34].

Current research seeks to identify anomalous activities based on time series prediction, and machine learning-based correlation analysis [26], or threat scores based on a static set of rules, e.g., HOLMES [36]. Given the lack of APT datasets, these techniques (1) do not consider modeling the aspects of stealthiness, completeness, and persistence that are paramount in the case of APTs and (2) can neither identify nor leverage correlations across multiple phases of an APT. For example, given that a reconnaissance phase is essential before establishing a foothold, detecting attack traffic at an earlier stage could be useful in identifying the latter stages of an APT.

The use of current datasets for APT detection is limiting in the sense that (a) there is no APT pattern in the datasets. The data used for machine learning-based APT research works utilize existing datasets such as CAIDA [46], NSL-KDD [20], consists of individual network attacks (probe, DoS, User to Root (U2R)), which are all performed simultaneously. (b) The analysis of recent datasets used for APT detection such as CICIDS 2017 [45] and CICIDS 2018 [16] shows that the attack vectors are limited to a few categories of attack - reconnaissance, privilege escalation, etc. In this work, we created a custom dataset, called the *DAPT 2020* (Dataset for APT 2020), by simulating behavior that mimics APTs on a cloud network for five days. We also collect and provide data from the initial phase when attack vectors for APT were not injected into the system, thus providing a baseline for modeling benign traffic on the network. On subsequent days, we captured attack traffic, representative of different phases of APTs by skilled attackers. APT properties like persistence, and slow & low movement are key characteristics of our dataset.

The key contributions of this research work are as follows:

- We provide dataset DAPT 2020 that captures the various aspects of real-world APT attacks. These include (1) attack behavior both at the interface and inside the network. The threat model used for the creation of the APT dataset incorporates the four main phases of an APT attack - reconnaissance, foothold establishment, lateral movement, and data exfiltration and (2) the traffic features in DAPT 2020 encodes several latent characteristics, such as adaptability and stealthiness, of APTs. To the best of our knowledge, this is the first dataset that captures network behavior spanning *all* the stages of an APT.
- We compare and contrast the properties of our dataset to three popular intrusion detection datasets – the CICIDS 2018 [16], the CICIDS 2017 [45], and the UNB 2015 [37] dataset. We highlight the missing aspects of the current datasets and show that our dataset fills the gaps. Further, we propose the new task of identifying a multi-step attack as opposed to classifying one-off anomalies. We believe that the use of the proposed dataset in the future will help to set new frontiers for developing ML models for real-world cybersecurity scenarios.
- Given the data imbalance in cyber attack datasets, where attack traffic is significantly less than the benign traffic data, we consider the use of state-of-the-art semi-supervised approaches for constructing a representation of the legitimate network behavior and then using it for identifying anomalies. We show that, across the various stages of an APT, these models are hardly effective in detecting attack traffic.

The rest of the paper has been organized as follows. We discuss the key characteristics of current datasets and machine learning models used in APT research in Sect. 2. The design of our dataset DAPT 2020, data collection methodology, and semi-supervised machine learning models used for benchmarking different phases of APT have been discussed in Sect. 3. In Sect. 4, we compare the performance of machine learning models on DAPT 2020, and existing datasets - CICIDS 2017 [45], CICIDS 2018 [16], and UNB 2015 [37]. We discuss the problem associated with the generalizability of existing datasets for APT detection and the need for better machine learning models in Sect. 5. Finally, we conclude the paper in Sect. 6 and provide directions for future research.

2   Related Work

Most of the current research focuses on detecting and mitigating the network intrusion based on pattern matching, signature-based, and anomaly-based IDSs. However, these IDSs fail to detect attack variants, that use the system vulnerabilities, before they damage the system. Although there has been some research done on APT attacks, most of them either describe and analyze the APT attacks that were disclosed such as Stuxnet [12], Duqu [7] and Flame [6]. Research works [14,44] consider APT attacks as a two-player game between attacker and defender. These studies do not discuss solutions for the automatic detection of APTs [31]. Many works that have been surveyed in [31,48] use the information correlation from various sources such as host-based events and network-based events to generate the evidence graphs. The research works are however limited by the type of attack vectors present in the network traffic.

2.1   Analysis on Existing Datasets

Table 1. Analysis of phases of APT attack covered by attack vectors of existing works involving APT, network intrusion, and anomaly detection in cybersecurity. The table compares attack phases covered by datasets UNB-15 [37], CICIDS 2017 [45], NSL-KDD [20], Mawi [25], ISCX [46], DARPA [17], HERITRIX [52], and DAPT 2020 (our dataset).

APT phase	Dataset							
	UNB-15	CICIDS	NSL-KDD	Mawi	ISCX	DARPA	HERITRIX	DAPT 2020
Normal traffic	✓	✓	✓	✓	✓	✓	✓	✓
Reconnaissance	✓	✓	✓		✓	✓		✓
Foothold establishment		✓	✓	✓	✓	✓	✓	✓
Lateral movement								✓
Data exfiltration								✓

Our analysis considered the datasets involving security intrusions and anomaly detection. For instance, Pang et al. [40] utilized deep anomaly detection based on deviation networks, and Moustafa et al. [37] used UNSW-NB15 intrusion detection dataset. We considered different phases of the APT attack as measurement metrics. As can be seen in the Table 1, DARPA [17] only covers three phases of APT attack. None of the existing datasets cover data exfiltration, which is

Table 2. Comparison between attack vectors of each dataset in terms of different attack vectors that is involved in APT attack. The table compares existence of every attack vectors by datasets UNB-15 [37], CICIDS 2018 [16] CICIDS 2017 [45], NSL-KDD [20], MAWI [25], ISCX [46], DARPA [17], HERITRIX [52], and DAPT 2020 (our dataset).

Attack	Dataset								
	UNB-15	CICIDS 2018	CICIDS 2017	NSL-KDD	MAWI	ISCX	DARPA	HERITRIX	DAPT 2020
Network scan	✓	✓	✓	✓	✓	✓	✓		✓
Web vulnerability scan	✓	✓							✓
Account bruteforce		✓	✓	✓	✓	✓	✓		✓
SQL injection		✓	✓	✓		✓			✓
Malware download	✓		✓						✓
Backdoor	✓	✓				✓			✓
Command injection	✓	✓	✓				✓	✓	✓
DoS	✓	✓	✓	✓	✓	✓	✓		✓
CSRF		✓	✓			✓			✓
Privilege escalation			✓		✓	✓		✓	✓

essential for the successful completion of an APT attack. Second, we analyzed the attack vectors utilized by different datasets, as described in the Table 2. The recent datasets such as UNB-15 lack attack vectors such as SQL Injection and Account Bruteforce. The datasets currently used for anomaly detection or machine learning-based research, targeting signature-based attacks or APT scenarios, lack a comprehensive set of attacks used for APT.

2.2 Anomaly Detection and Machine Learning Based APT Detection

Machine learning has been found and proven by many researchers as one of the promising solutions towards detecting APT attacks. Qu *et al.* [41] have proposed an autoencoder model, with the gated-recurrent unit (GRU) as the basic unit, trained in an unsupervised approach towards detecting anomalies in web log data. They compare the accuracy of their model with Long Short Term Memory (LSTM) and Support Vector Machine (SVM) models. They used a clustering approach to reduce the feature space before giving it to the autoencoder. Bohara *et al.* in [8] presented an unsupervised clustering approach on combined network and host logs to find any malicious activity. They claimed their approach can detect network scan attacks, flooding attacks, and the presence of malware on a host. Both these solutions embraced unsupervised machine learning approaches and are susceptible to high false positives and false negatives. Further, Bohara *et al.* [8] uses a clustering approach that is affected by the initial seed and number of clusters. Du *et al.* [22] proposed a DeepLog framework for anomaly detection based on system log where LSTM was utilized to derive a model trained on normal patterns with the ability to detect abnormal activities of DDoS attacks. Kumar et al. [30] proposed a framework to detect security intrusions using a hybrid approach of rules and machine learning techniques. Marchetti *et al.* [32] proposed a supervised statistical approach based on network traffic logs and access information to detect APT activities after establishing foothold to exfil-tration attempts including lateral movement and maintaining access. Siddiqui *et al.* [47] have used K-Nearest Neighbor (KNN) machine-learning algorithm to detect the activities about the lateral movement and exfiltration stages of an APT attack. Cappers *et al.* in [10] proposed a semi-supervised machine learning approach to detect APT activities from establishing a foothold stage to data ex-filtration stage by contextual analysis of network traffic alerts.

3   DAPT 2020 Dataset Design

A key component lacking in current APT research is an APT dataset. A pri-mary reason for this shortcoming is the legitimate skepticism amongst corporate organizations to share network attack data as it may reveal important aspects of the company. Further, the fear of disclosing personally identifiable information (PIO), and breaching the customer confidentiality agreement prevents compa-nies from sharing this data. Hence, we try to construct an artificial dataset with characteristics of APT behavior as DAPT 2020.

In this section, we first provide an overview of the system-setup for facilitating data-collection. We then describe the data-collection process, giving an overview of the timeline and highlight the tools used for data-collection. Finally, we discuss state-of-the-art techniques that can be leveraged to distinguish between benign and malicious traffic.

3.1   System Setup

We utilized VMWare ESXi physical servers to host the virtual machines (VMs) with different services typical of an enterprise cloud network. As can be seen in the Fig. 1, the Public VM comprised vulnerable services such as mutilli-dae [39], Damn Vulnerable Web Application (DVWA) [23], Metasploitable [43], and BadStore [50]. We utilized Snort, Network-based Intrusion Detection Sys-tem (NIDS) [42] for checking the malicious traffic signatures. Each service was hosted as a separate Docker [33] container. The private VM was used to host services such as Samba, Wordpress website, FTP, MySQL, nexus (repository management). The private and public VMs were connected over the private net-work. Additionally, each VM had a packet and log capture feature. The ELK stack [13] based log server was used for log storage and filtering. The network and host logs were periodically shipped to the Log Server using filebeat agent as shown in Fig. 1.

3.2   Data Collection

To mimic normal traffic seen on read-world cyber systems, a group of users was provided user and (some with) administrative credentials, for accessing public

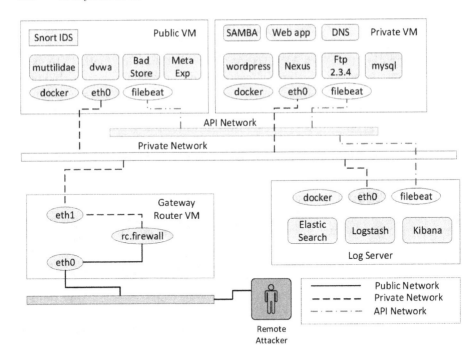

Fig. 1. System set used for construction of DAPT 2020 dataset. The attacker can access only public services exposed via firewall. Log Server (ELK Cluster) is used for collection of network and host logs.

Table 3. Table with details on data collection on a multi-tenant cloud system with known and unknown vulnerabilities

Day	Activity	Tools used	Details
Day 1, 8:00 AM–6:00 PM	Normal traffic	ping, dig, GET, POST, curl, browsing, files upload, download	Baseline normal traffic based on user activities
Day 2, 8:00 AM–6:00 PM	Reconnaissance	nmap, webscarab, sqlmap, dirbuster, nikto, burpsuite, application account discovery tools	Reconnaissance on public network, identification of vulnerabilities, directory structure, weak authentication, and authorization
Day 3, 8:00 AM–6:00 PM	Foothold establishment	PHP reverse shell, netcat, SQL vulnerability exploitation (sqlmap), XSS exploitation, authentication bypass, metasploitable	PHP reverse shell via DVWA, file upload, adding of malicious users was performed on badstore
Day 4, 8:00 AM–6:00 PM	Lateral movement	Nmap scan on local network, vsftpd 2.3.4 vulnerability, weak ssh authentication, mysql script for CVE-2012-2122, metasploit	Exploration of internal network from compromised VMs (Public VM), and obtaining foothold on critical local systems
Day 5, 8:00 AM–6:00 PM	Data exfiltration	Data exfiltration to C&C, SMB vulnerability CVE-2017-7494 used to obtain elevated privileges, Google Drive, PyExfil, ftp, scp	FTP put method from local machine to remote server, wput to remote location using anonymous user, scp large files to remote server, web based uploads to Google Drive

and private services of the network. They performed routine business operations throughout the week. For instance, admin performed some updates to a Word-Press website, organized files, folders, users. On Monday, we ensured that no attack traffic was present on the network to generate a baseline for normal traffic. Then, as highlighted in Table 3, various attack methods were employed by our internal Red Team (team of experienced cyber-attackers). They performed a chain of attacks that mimic real-world APT attacks similar to the ones described by Alshamrani *et al.* [1]. On Tuesday, the Red Team attempted exploration (e.g. scanning and fingerprinting) of software present on public services. The team exploited vulnerabilities present on public services. On Wednesday the team used attack scripts and known attack tools such as metasploitable to establish a foothold and gain elevated privileges on the services present on the public network. In the next phase of the attack on Thursday, the Red Team employed lateral movement to exploit critical services in the network such as SMB, and FTP. Finally, the team used data exfiltration methods to send the data to external google drives, and FTP server on Friday. This completed the APT attack. Note, that an actual APT attack takes place over a longer duration, but the attack phases are quite similar to the experimental analysis performed by our internal team. A detailed description of attack tools used and findings during each phase of the attack are present on our public Gitlab repository [38].

Table 4. Comparison of attack methods employed in DAPT 2020 dataset against methods employed by real-world APT attacks - APT41 [21] and Target APT Breach [51]

APT phases	DAPT 2020	APT41	Target breach	RSA SecureID
Reconnaissance	Network scan			
	Application scan			
	Account Bruteforce	✓		
Establish foothold	CSRF	✓		
	SQL injection	✓	✓	
	Malware download		✓	
	Backdoor	✓		✓
	Reverse shell	✓	✓	
	Command injection			
Lateral movement	Internal scanning	✓	✓	
	Account discovery		✓	
	Password dumping	✓	✓	✓
	Credential theft	✓	✓	✓
	Creation of user accounts	✓		
	Privelege escalation	✓		✓
Data exfiltration	Data theft	✓	✓	✓

The normal users (students with basic knowledge of website maintenance and access), used shopping interface to checkout items, browse different options, create posts on the website, add comments on particular items, etc. The normal user operations continued over next few days. Attackers (advanced penetration testers) were instructed to be as stealthy as possible and perform attacks in a fashion that prevents any alarms triggered by security tools. The attackers were given access and used tools, techniques, and procedures (TTPs) similar to state of the art APT attacks to simulate APT attack. The data was collected from all the network interfaces in the form of (pcap) files, as well as logs from each host.

In particular, the host logs we collected were as follows:

– Log of system events (Syslog)
– MySQL access log
– Auditd host IDS logs
– Apache Access Logs
– Authentication Logs
– Logs from services - wordpress, docker, samba, ftp
– DNS logs

Constructing a dataset that represents real-world APT attacks is crucial to the success of the dataset and the models generated using that dataset. Our dataset, DAPT 2020, has been constructed by studying different APT attack groups and their methods. Table 4 compares the attack methods employed for constructing our dataset, DAPT 2020, with the attack methods of employed in real-world APT attacks.

3.3 Semi-supervised Models for APT Detection

Understanding the normal behavior of systems within a network plays a crucial role in defending against APTs [1]. By developing a baseline for the normal behavior of a system, any deviation from this baseline, indicative of abnormal behavior, can be effectively identified. Semi-supervised approaches prevalent in anomaly detection leverage this idea to distinguish between normal and attack traffic at test time [9,11]. An advantage of using such semi-supervised techniques is that they are robust to the issue of data imbalance in network-traffic datasets. In real-world settings, which motivate the construction of such data-sets, the number of attack packets is considerably less than the number of normal traffic packets. For example, the proportion of users doing regular activities on a website like Google or Amazon or Facebook *vs.* the users trying to exploit it, is quite less. According to a study by F-Secure [5], 22% of companies did not detect a single attack in 2018 over 12 months, 20% of respondents detected only one type of attack over that period, whereas 31% companies reported 2–5 attacks. Although data to learn normal behavior is abundant, designing a full-fledged supervised classifier that can detect anomalies well, is quite challenging.

Our dataset consists of traffic data on an interconnected network of systems and is rich in contextual information. Regardless of the day on which the attacks are executed, the amount of attack traffic is a small fraction of the overall data. Thus, it makes sense for us to use semi-supervised learning approaches discussed in the literature. We will now discuss a few of these machine learning models that act as a benchmark for our proposed dataset and also the existing models which are considered later in our experiments.

- **One-Class Support Vector Machines (1-SVM)** are known to be particularly effective in scenarios where there is a large amount of normal traffic and a small fraction of anomalous traffic data [24,35]. The idea is to train the model on the labeled examples of the class that has more data. In our case, we trained the 1-SVM model on the abundant normal network traffic data. We then, at test time, using a pre-defined threshold, decide whether a reconstruction error is large enough to classify it as an anomaly.
- **Stacked Auto Encoder (SAE)** - Auto-encoders are a specific kind of feedforward neural network [49] that are meant to find a compact latent-space representation of the input which can be leveraged for reconstruction. Autoencoders have one hidden layer and compression occurs between the input and hidden layer while reconstruction occurs between the hidden and the output layer. In Stacked Auto-encoders, the compression function followed by the reconstruction is done with a deep neural network as opposed to a single non-linear layer. During training, the output of an SAE is forced to mimic the input; thus, the loss function seeks to minimize the distance between the original input and the reconstructed output. We first train an SAE on normal traffic data, followed by testing on both normal and anomalous data. The expectation is that although SAE can accurately reconstruct the normal data, it fails to do so effectively for the abnormal data and has higher reconstruction error [2]. This makes it easy for a classifier to detect anomalous network traffic data by comparing the reconstruction error to a pre-defined threshold.
- **Stacked Auto Encoder with Long Short-Term Memory (LSTM-SAE)** - While a regular stacked auto-encoders have been used in many research works, the SAE is not capable of detecting contextual anomalies, which is of great significance in the context of APTs. This is because the input layers of an SAE only accept a single network packet as input. To solve this issue, we use a stacked auto-encoder that uses LSTM cells instead of hidden layer cells of SAEs. LSTMs, which have been successful in time-series analysis [4]. LSTM allows us to consider data across multiple time steps. The modified SAE, termed as LSTM-SAE, helps us to compress network traffic packets in multiple consecutive time-steps and then, reconstruct it. By using the same mechanism of training on abundant normal data and testing on both attack and normal data, we can detect attacks that are executed in parts, i.e. spread across multiple packets. This provides both a good benchmark for our dataset and it is a promising first-step for contextual anomaly detection.

4   Evaluation

In this section, we compare the performance of the different models, mentioned above, on three existing datasets – the CICIDS 2017 [45], CICIDS 2018 [16], UNB

2015 [37] – and our proposed dataset DAPT 2020. The goal is to show that similar semi-supervised learning methods, i.e. similar semi-supervised architectures with similar training hyper-parameters, can detect anomalies better in the case of existing data-sets in comparison to detecting anomalies in our dataset DAPT 2020.

The anomaly detection models we have used are based on the Stacked Auto-Encoder (SAE), the LSTM Stacked Auto-Encoder (LSTM-SAE), and a single-class Support Vector Machine. The key idea behind using these models for anomaly detection briefly highlighted in Sect. 3 is to train these models on the normal traffic data on the network. At test time, given an input, we pass it thorough the auto-encoder and check if the normalized reconstruction error is above a certain threshold. If so, we classify it as an anomalous traffic packet. Otherwise, we classify it as normal traffic.

A metric to gauge the effectiveness of anomaly detection systems in settings that have class imbalance issues, such as anomaly prediction in the context of cyber-attacks, is the Precision-Recall (PR) curve as opposed to more popular measures such as accuracy and Receiver Operating Characteristics (ROC) [19]. First, given that attack representation is often less than 2% in the test-set, even a naive classifier that classifies all data to the majority class will have a 98% accuracy. Further, the difference between algorithms on a dataset (or between datasets using the same algorithm) is harder to reason about within the 2% scale. Second, although both the ROC and the PR curve use the Recall (or the True Positive Rate), ROC uses the False Positive Rate (FPR) in comparison to the PR curve's Precision. The FPR rate is less sensitive to changes in the number of false positives (i.e. normal traffic being classified as attacks) while Precision looks at only the set of samples that are predicted to be positive. Thus, it provides a much better metric when a particular class is severely underrepresented in comparison to another class. A detailed discussion on this topic can be found in [19]. Third, comparing the performance of an algorithm on different data-sets using accuracy or the ROC curve becomes quite misleading in our context because of the different degree to which anomalies are under-represented in the data. For example, the ratio of attack traffic in the case of brute-force attacks for CICIDS 2018 is $\approx$22% while for UNB 2015 it is $\approx$14%. Hence, the baselines for the two datasets (i.e., a naive classifier that classifies everything to the majority class label) will have 75% and 86% accuracy respectively. Hence putting them side by side on the accuracy table or the AUC of a ROC curve does not help quantify the effectiveness of an algorithm to classify the data. For completeness, we will discuss the AUC-ROC and AUC-PR data in the Subsect. 4.4. We now briefly discuss how the PR-curves were constructed and should be interpreted.

In our setting, the model outputs a confidence value of p after normalizing the reconstruction error across all test examples between $[0, 1]$. When the reconstruction error is large, the value of p is close to 1. Thus, p indicates the confidence with which the model predicts an input as an anomaly (i.e. belongs to class 1). To plot a point in the PR-curve, we first set a threshold of τ. We then, for each test inputs, find p, and if $p < \tau$ we classify it as normal traffic (and

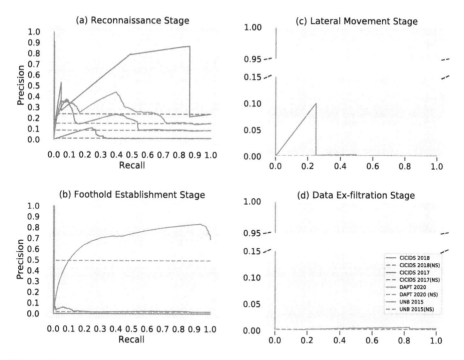

Fig. 2. Precision-Recall (PR) curves for detecting attacks across the various stages of an APT for the various datasets using the Stacked Auto-encoder (SAE).

as anomalous traffic otherwise). By doing this for all test inputs, we can come up with a confusion matrix (that showcases the True/False Positives/Negatives). Finally, we obtain the Precision and Recall for the particular τ and plot it on the PR-curve. The ideal classifier should be able to correctly predict the test label of each input with complete confidence, i.e. for anomalies, it outputs $p = 1$, while for normal, it predicts $p = 0$. Such a classifier plots the line $y = 1$ and then stretches from $(-1, 1)$ to the point $(1, \text{frac. of anomalous examples})$ in the PR curve. On the other hand, a No-Skill (NS) classifier that outputs $p = 1$ on all input data can be plotted using the line,

$$y = \text{Precison} = \frac{TP}{TP + NP} = \frac{\#(\text{Anomalous Traffic})}{\#(\text{Dataset})}$$

where $\#(\cdot)$ denotes the cardinality. For all our PR-curves that follow the no-skill classifier's performance is shown using dotted lines and, in the legend, indexed using the suffix NS. In the PR-space, a curve that is higher compared to another curve or closer to the top-right corner of the unit-square (with corners at $(0, 0)$ and $(1, 1)$) is considered to represent better anomaly detection.

As opposed to considering the detection of anomalies as a whole, which is common in all existing works, we break the anomalies down into the four stages of APTs– Reconnaissance, Foothold Establishment, Lateral Movement, and Data

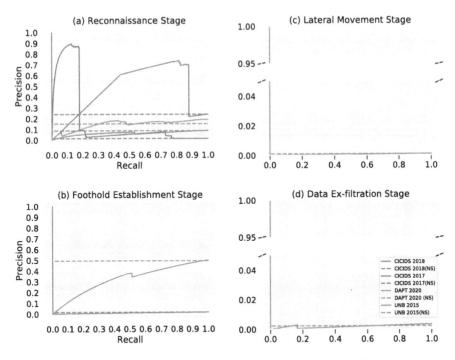

Fig. 3. Precision-Recall (PR) curves for detecting attacks across the various stages of an APT for the various datasets using the Stacked Auto-encoder with LSTM cells (LSTM-SAE).

Exfiltration. This helps us highlight the various characteristics of attacks (data imbalance ratios, lack of data) across the different APT stages that make the semi-supervised learning task difficult. We are also able to show that even in the context of existing data, the abundance of attack data in one-phase helps the accuracy of the overall anomaly detection system, which may be highly unreliable in another context.

We divide the results of our experiments into three subsections– one for each of the semi-supervised learning methods. Due to the lack of particular attack vectors in each of the existing datasets, highlighted in Table 1, UNB 2015, CICIDS 2017, and CICIDS 2018 data-sets are only used to detect attack in the Reconnaissance and the Foothold Establishment stages. Each row of figures represents the PR-curves for a particular anomaly detection model and are arranged as per the detection result of reconnaissance data on the left and data-exfiltration on the right. The ordering is the representation of the way APT attacks progress through the system.

Attack Vector Details. The following attack vectors were selected for benchmarking models on the different stages present in the DAPT 2020 dataset:

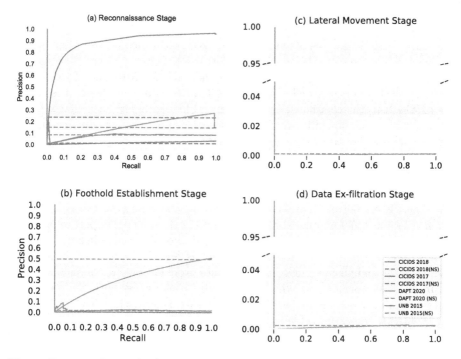

Fig. 4. Precision-Recall (PR) curves for detecting attacks across the various stages of an APT for the various datasets using 1-class Support Vector Machine (1-SVM).

1. Reconnaissance - Web Application Scan, Port Scan, Account Discovery
2. Foothold Establishment - Directory Bruteforce, SQL Injection, Malware Download
3. Lateral Movement - Port Scan (on a private network), backdoor, SQL Injection (on a private network)
4. Data Exfiltration - exfiltration to a remote FTP server, Google Drive upload.

The training set for individual attack stages comprised of all normal traffic data seen on weekdays when attack vectors belonging to the particular attack stage was absent. On the other hand, the test set comprised of all the traffic data–both attack and normal–on days attack vectors indicative of the attack stage was executed. For example, training data for lateral movement in DAPT 2020 consisted of normal data from Monday, Tuesday, Wednesday, and Friday (days on which there was no lateral movement), whereas the test set consisted of normal and attack data from Thursday.

The results are shown in Fig. 2, 3, and 4, mostly portray the failure of the semi-supervised system as being able to detect attack vectors in APT scenarios. Further, the data imbalance also makes it hard for supervised learners to perform well in this context. We sincerely hope that the benchmarking results act as an encouragement for the research community to propose better methods that are better at anomaly detection in the context of real-world APTs.

4.1 Anomaly Detection with SAE

The anomaly detection results using the Stacked Auto-Encoder (SAE) are shown in Fig. 2. As can be seen, the classifier performs satisfactorily in only two settings – (1) detecting reconnaissance attacks on the CICIDS 2018 and (2) detecting foothold establishment attacks in our DAPT 2020 dataset. Beyond these cases, the AUC-PR of the classifiers, as shown in Table 5 is highly unsatisfactory and often as bad as the no-skill classifier. We do not compare the results for different datasets across the various stages of the APT.

Reconnaissance. The anomaly detection on CICIDS 2018, for which the no-skill classifier has a precision value of 0.23, corresponding to the fraction of anomalies, is far better than on any of the other datasets with the highest precision value of 0.87 for some threshold. For the other datasets, performance on our DAPT 2020 and the UNB 2015 dataset do not differ significantly. This is because the baseline of the no-skill classifier is higher in our case as opposed to UNB 2015 and thus, similar improvements produce the PR curves plotted in Figure 2(a). Performance on the CICIDS 2017 is the worst with the maximum precision value reaching to barely 0.1. Not surprisingly, the AUC-PR for the CICIDS 2017, shown in Table 5, is the worst for this setting.

Foothold Establishment. The fraction of attack data in the context of Foothold Establishment is significantly less in the existing datasets with only a section of the brute force and sparse SQL Injection attack vectors in the haystack of normal data. In our case, nearly 50% of the traffic consists of attacks that try to gain a foothold in the network. The performance of SAE in the context of our dataset dominates the performance on other datasets by a significant margin. Further, the scanty traffic in the other datasets is not easily distinguishable from the normal data, resulting in the SAE behaving as bad as a no-skill classifier in this setting.

Lateral Movement and Data Ex-Filtration. The y-scale of the graph in this setting ranges show activity between $[0, 0.15]$ instead of the usual $[0, 1]$ scale in the context of other attacks. The plot acts as proof to show that attack data representing lateral movement exists in the dataset. The performance of the SAE is extremely poor, reaching a maximum precision of 0.1. As can be observed, re-scaling the axis is needed for all plots on the detection of lateral movement and data-ex-filtration data, but the performance of other models deteriorates even further.

4.2 Anomaly Detection with LSTM-SAE

The anomaly detection results using the LSTM-based Stacked Auto-encoder (LSTM-SAE) are plotted in Fig. 3. The results for LSTM-SAE is only promising for the CICIDS 2017 and the CICIDS 2018 dataset in the context of reconnaissance attacks. A more detailed discussion follows.

Reconnaissance. An interesting observation, in comparison to the performance of SAE on the CICIDS-2017 dataset, is that the performance of LSTM-SAE shows significant improvement, jumping from a max precision value of 0.1 in the former case to a value of ≈0.9 in the latter plot. This is, to an extent, indicative that there exists contextual information that is the CICIDS-2018 dataset that can be leveraged by LSTM-SAEs to better detect anomalies. This might result because of a particular pattern that was used to inject attack data for this dataset. Looking at the performance on the other datasets, it seems that the addition of contextual information makes the distinct representation of the attack vectors difficult, making them close to normal representation and in turn, reducing the effectiveness of anomaly detection.

Foothold Establishment. In this setting, the LSTM-SAE turns out to be the worst classifier. It is as bad as using a no-skill classifier for all the datasets concerned. As can be observed from the data, compared to SAE or 1-SVM, even with a sufficiently large fraction of attack data, it cannot perform any better. This gives a clear indication that the use of contextual information (of up to 3 timesteps) dilutes attack data for our dataset. We discuss this further when analyzing on the AUC values for the PR curves.

Lateral Movement and Data Ex-Filtration. The LSTM-SAEs performance is worse than that of SAE on the Lateral Movement and Data Ex-filtration data compared to other stages of the APT attack. This shows that the distribution of contextualized attack vectors in these stages is almost the same as that of normal traffic.

4.3   Anomaly Detection with 1-SVM

In Fig. 4, we highlight the performance of a one-class Support Vector Machine on the different data-sets. Other than the case of detecting Foothold establishment attacks on our dataset DAPT 2020, the 1-SVM performs poorly in all the cases.

Reconnaissance. The learning classifier performs as bad as the no-skill classifier for all the datasets except CICIDS 2018. In the case of CICIDS 2018, it performs quite well compared to CICIDS 2017, UNB 2015, and DAPT 2020 dataset. It essentially implies that for the CICIDS 2018 dataset, it essentially means that the classifier can identify the anomalous traffic correctly. This can be explained by the fact that a large percent of attack traffic in CICIDS included quite observable attempts by the attacker to perform reconnaissance. The classifier is, however, not able to identify the anomalous events in DAPT 2020 and other datasets, given that the percentage of attack traffic is quite low.

Foothold Establishment. The 1-SVM performs the best for detecting attacks in the foothold establishment stage in our dataset going up to a 0.9 on precision value while it performs almost as bad as the no-skill classifiers for the other datasets. Since foothold establishment is a key stage associated with any APT attack, this was expected behavior.

Lateral Movement and Data Ex-Filtration. Similar to the anomaly detection behavior seen in the case of SAE and LSTM-SAE, the PR curves for the 1-SVM show extremely poor performance for detecting attacks in the two final stages of APTs. This shows that attacks were quite stealthy and almost identical to the normal traffic. It is clear that the reliable detection of these attack phases on an actual APT attack is quite difficult with existing anomaly detection models.

4.4   Analysis of Performance on AUC

Stacked autoencoder performed well on reconnaissance, and foothold establishment phase, whereas 1-SVM performed better on lateral movement, and data-exfiltration phase. LSTM-SAE performed quite poorly on all phases of APT. AUC-PR values are quite low suggesting anomalies to be sparsely distributed.

We enumerate the Area Under Curve - Receiver Operating Characteristics (AUC-ROC), and AUC Precision-Recall (AUC-PR) values of the classifiers on the dataset UNB 2015, CICIDS 2017, CICIDS 2018, and DAPT 2020 in Table 5. AUC-ROC summarizes the ROC curves of true positives against false positives, while AUC-PR is a summarizes the curve of precision against the recall. If the AUC-ROC value is quite high (close to 1), it implies good performance, whereas AUC-ROC value close to 0.5 means a random ranking of the objects. The choice of performance metric AUC-ROC and AUC-PR depends on the goal of the anomaly detection method. AUC-ROC is used because of good interpretability, however, if the anomaly detection mechanism is sensitive to the performance on the positive class as opposed to negative class, AUC-PR is a good performance metric for anomaly detection. If the anomalies are distributed unevenly in the dataset, the value of AUC-PR is generally low.

Reconnaissance. The SAE model performed quite well on most of the datasets in the reconnaissance phase, achieving *0.601* AUC-ROC value, in case of UNB 2015, 0.832 in case of CICIDS 2018, and 0.641 in the case of DAPT 2020 dataset. Surprisingly, the SAE-LSTM showcased better AUC value compared to SAE, and 1-SVM on CICIDS dataset. The AUC-PR values were consistently low for all the algorithms in the reconnaissance phase. This means the attack distribution was quite sparse during the reconnaissance phase and thereby, difficult to detect.

Foothold Establishment. The SAE showed good performance in the case of DAPT 2020 for foothold establishment (0.846). These results are on the lines of PR curves observed in the previous section for the foothold establishment stage. The AUC-PR values for foothold establishment are higher for DAPT 2020

Table 5. AUC-ROC and AUC-PR results for machine learning models - SAE, SAE-LSTM, 1-SVM.

Dataset	AUC-ROC			AUC-PR		
	Reconnaissance			Reconnaissance		
	SAE	SAE-LSTM	1-SVM	SAE	SAE-LSTM	1-SVM
UNB 2015	**0.601**	0.352	0.489	0.158	0.061	0.079
CICIDS 2017	0.499	**0.727**	0.66	0.0263	0.173	0.018
CICIDS 2018	**0.832**	0.799	0.99	0.592	0.457	0.88
DAPT 2020	**0.641**	0.525	0.54	0.262	0.143	0.15
Dataset	Foothold establishment			Foothold establishment		
	SAE	SAE-LSTM	1-SVM	SAE	SAE-LSTM	1-SVM
UNB 2015	**0.602**	0.09	0.547	0.0280	0.009	0.019
CICIDS 2017	**0.365**	0.34	0.670	0.000001	0.00001	0.00018
CICIDS 2018	**0.674**	0.665	0.540	0.0001	0.00001	0.000001
DAPT 2020	**0.846**	0.386	0.058	0.498	0.323	0.313
Dataset	Lateral movement			Lateral movement		
	SAE	SAE-LSTM	1-SVM	SAE	SAE-LSTM	1-SVM
UNB 2015	NA	NA	NA	NA	NA	NA
CICIDS 2017	NA	NA	NA	NA	NA	NA
CICIDS 2018	NA	NA	NA	NA	NA	NA
DAPT 2020	**0.634**	0.28	0.25	0.0136	0.0006	0.0006
Dataset	Data exfiltration			Data exfiltration		
	SAE	SAE-LSTM	1-SVM	SAE	SAE-LSTM	1-SVM
UNB 2015	NA	NA	NA	NA	NA	NA
CICIDS 2017	NA	NA	NA	NA	NA	NA
CICIDS 2018	NA	NA	NA	NA	NA	NA
DAPT 2020	**0.685**	0.386	0.298	0.0034	0.0027	0.0015

dataset compared to other datasets, since attack traffic was bit higher compared to other datasets, 0.323 for LSTM-SAE, and 0.313 for 1-SVM.

Lateral Movement and Data Ex-Filtration. The foothold establishment and lateral movement phases were missing on the existing datasets. The different machine learning models when evaluated on DAPT 2020 consistently showed poor performance, for both lateral movement and data exfiltration. Moreover, the consistently low values of all unsupervised learning algorithms on these phases of APT show that the attack vectors employed in our dataset are highly stealthy and difficult to detect using existing classifiers.

5 Discussion

As already highlighted, the availability of data on APT is difficult because of (1) privacy concerns pertaining to an organization and its customers and (2) spending effort in creating a data-set like DAPT 2020 is both time-consuming and expensive. Given that we now propose the DAPT 2020 dataset, it is natural to consider the use of data-augmentation techniques prevalent in the machine learning community [3]. However, there are two concerns in using data-augmentation techniques. First, the current dataset reflects an APT attack with thin lines between normal and abnormal behaviors of the systems within the network. As a result, ensuring that augmentation of the normal traffic still represents normal behavior of the systems is quiet challenging. Second, unlike regular intrusion detection datasets, this dataset represents an APT attack where in consecutive attack vectors are inter-related. Data augmentation can potentially affect these dependency relations with the generated attack data failing to capture the APT attackers' movement in the network. Further, GANs are known to exacerbate biases and thus, generated data may induce mode collapse, repeating a particular patterns present in the attack data to generate synthetic attack traffic, in turn reducing its rich diversity [27]. We believe, the effectiveness of data augmentation in regards to APT traffic needs to be investigated, and we intend to move in this direction in near future. We plan to consider GAN based models to identify better machine learning models in context of APT attacks.

While machine learning models are known to be less effective when test data is out-of-distribution (OOD), the problem amplifies further in the context of cyber-security. Each system is highly specific to the software it uses, the inputs (or outputs) it expects (or generates), the traffic patterns seen etc. Hence, a model trained on a particular dataset might not be as effective when used in a different context. DAPT 2020 helps bridge this gap and provides motivation for the development of machine learning technologies suitable for APT attack detection.

6 Conclusion

Advanced Persistent Threats are one of the most challenging attacks to defend against. Several machine learning research works have tried to address the APT detection problem. They are, however, limited by the attack vectors, and the attack phases critical for an APT attack. We propose a new DAPT 2020 dataset, and benchmark existing anomaly detection models on our dataset. The performance of anomaly detection models in terms of precision-recall (PR) values, AUC-ROC, and AUC-PR values is consistently low. This shows that reliable detection of APT attacks using existing machine learning models is very difficult, and more effort needs to be invested towards creating better learning models for APT detection. Further, a key component that is required for defending against APTs is a correlation model that correlates the anomalies detected. We believe this DAPT 2020 dataset instigates development of fine correlation models that help detect a threat in its entirety and not just the individual attack vectors. The code and dataset for this research work can be found at https://gitlab.thothlab.org/Advanced-Persistent-Threat/apt-2020/tree/master (along-with a detailed description of DAPT-20 [38]).

Acknowledgement. This research is supported in part by following research grants: Naval Research Lab N0017319-1-G002, NSF DGE-1723440, OAC-1642031. Sailik Sengupta is supported by the IBM Ph.D. Fellowship.

A   Appendix

A.1   APT Attack Phases

The detailed description of different APT phases are as follows:

Reconnaissance

- **Scan Applications** - Nessus, Web Scarab, Burp Suite. Find vulnerabilities such as XSS, XSRF, SQL Injection etc.
- **Scan Network** - NMap, Portsweep, Mscan, Satan, Ipsweep, Saint. Find systems' fingerprints, network architecture information etc. Firewall should log deny event. If multiple denies are seen against unique destination ports from the same origin host within a small windows of time, it is safe to assume that some sort of port scanning activity is taking place.

Establish Foothold

- **Download or Install Malware** - Scanbox, Backdoor Sogu, PoisonIvy, Key-Loggers.
- **R2L** - Guess_Password, Ftp_Write, Imap, Phf, Multihop, Warezmaster, Warezclient, SpyXlock, Xsnoop, Snmpguess, Snmpgetattack, Httptunnel, Sendmail, Named.
- **C&C Communication** - Send communication to external server that the malware has been installed. Monitor network traffic originating from a system to an external server, after a download of a file or similar network activity.

Lateral Movement

- **Credential Compromise** - Key Loggers, Hash retrieval, LDAP, Metasploit.
- **Privilege Escalation (U2R)** - Buffer_Overflow, Loadmodule, Rootkit, Perl, Sqlattack, Xterm, PS.

Internal Reconnaissance. Same as Reconnaissance above, just from different source in search of data. IP range might be probed for port 1433 in case of enumerating SQL servers. Ports 135–139 are usually probed by attackers when in search of network shares.

Data Exfiltration. Uploading to Google Drive, Dropbox, AWS or any such cloud. Need to baseline against the normal activity of a system.

Cover Up. Deletion of log files, modification of log files etc. Needs host based intrusion detection agent. OUT OF SCOPE for current research.

A.2   APT Feature Description

We collected the following features from network and host logs. The details of features extracted extracted from the data collected are present in the Table 6.

Table 6. APT20 feature description

fl_dur	Flow duration
tot_fw_pk	Total packets in the forward direction
tot_bw_pk	Total packets in the backward direction
tot_l_fw_pkt	Total size of packet in forward direction
fw_pkt_l_max	Maximum size of packet in forward direction
fw_pkt_l_min	Minimum size of packet in forward direction
fw_pkt_l_avg	Average size of packet in forward direction
fw_pkt_l_std	Standard deviation size of packet in forward direction
Bw_pkt_l_max	Maximum size of packet in backward direction
Bw_pkt_l_min	Minimum size of packet in backward direction
Bw_pkt_l_avg	Mean size of packet in backward direction
Bw_pkt_l_std	Standard deviation size of packet in backward direction
fl_byt_s	Flow byte rate that is number of packets transferred per second
fl_pkt_s	Flow packets rate that is number of packets transferred per second
fl_iat_avg	Average time between two flows
fl_iat_std	Standard deviation time two flows
fl_iat_max	Maximum time between two flows
fl_iat_min	Minimum time between two flows
fw_iat_tot	Total time between two packets sent in the forward direction
fw_iat_avg	Mean time between two packets sent in the forward direction
fw_iat_std	Standard deviation time between two packets sent in the forward direction
fw_iat_max	Maximum time between two packets sent in the forward direction
fw_iat_min	Minimum time between two packets sent in the forward direction
bw_iat_tot	Total time between two packets sent in the backward direction
bw_iat_avg	Mean time between two packets sent in the backward direction

(continued)

Table 6. (*continued*)

fl_dur	Flow duration
bw_iat_std	Standard deviation time between two packets sent in the backward direction
bw_iat_max	Maximum time between two packets sent in the backward direction
bw_iat_min	Minimum time between two packets sent in the backward direction
fw_psh_flag	Number of times the PSH flag was set in packets travelling in the forward direction (0 for UDP)
bw_psh_flag	Number of times the PSH flag was set in packets travelling in the backward direction (0 for UDP)
fw_urg_flag	Number of times the URG flag was set in packets travelling in the forward direction (0 for UDP)
bw_urg_flag	Number of times the URG flag was set in packets travelling in the backward direction (0 for UDP)
fw_hdr_len	Total bytes used for headers in the forward direction
bw_hdr_len	Total bytes used for headers in the forward direction
fw_pkt_s	Number of forward packets per second
bw_pkt_s	Number of backward packets per second
pkt_len_min	Minimum length of a flow
pkt_len_max	Maximum length of a flow
pkt_len_avg	Mean length of a flow
pkt_len_std	Standard deviation length of a flow
pkt_len_va	Minimum inter-arrival time of packet
fin_cnt	Number of packets with FIN
syn_cnt	Number of packets with SYN
rst_cnt	Number of packets with RST
pst_cnt	Number of packets with PUSH
ack_cnt	Number of packets with ACK
urg_cnt	Number of packets with URG
cwe_cnt	Number of packets with CWE
ece_cnt	Number of packets with ECE
down_up_ratio	Download and upload ratio
pkt_size_avg	Average size of packet
fw_seg_avg	Average size observed in the forward direction
bw_seg_avg	Average size observed in the backward direction
fw_byt_blk_avg	Average number of bytes bulk rate in the forward direction
fw_pkt_blk_avg	Average number of packets bulk rate in the forward direction
fw_blk_rate_avg	Average number of bulk rate in the forward direction

(*continued*)

Table 6. (*continued*)

fl_dur	Flow duration
bw_byt_blk_avg	Average number of bytes bulk rate in the backward direction
bw_pkt_blk_avg	Average number of packets bulk rate in the backward direction
bw_blk_rate_avg	Average number of bulk rate in the backward direction
subfl_fw_pk	The average number of packets in a sub flow in the forward direction
subfl_fw_byt	The average number of bytes in a sub flow in the forward direction
subfl_bw_pkt	The average number of packets in a sub flow in the backward direction
subfl_bw_byt	The average number of bytes in a sub flow in the backward direction
fw_win_byt	Number of bytes sent in initial window in the forward direction
bw_win_byt	Number of bytes sent in initial window in the backward direction
fw_act_pk	Number of packets with at least 1 byte of TCP data payload in the forward direction
fw_seg_min	Minimum segment size observed in the forward direction
atv_avg	Mean time a flow was active before becoming idle
atv_std	Standard deviation time a flow was active before becoming idle
atv_max	Maximum time a flow was active before becoming idle
atv_min	Minimum time a flow was active before becoming idle
idl_avg	Mean time a flow was idle before becoming active
idl_std	Standard deviation time a flow was idle before becoming active
idl_max	Maximum time a flow was idle before becoming active
idl_min	Minimum time a flow was idle before becoming active

References

1. Alshamrani, A., Myneni, S., Chowdhary, A., Huang, D.: A survey on advanced persistent threats: techniques, solutions, challenges, and research opportunities. IEEE Commun. Surv. Tutorials **21**(2), 1851–1877 (2019)
2. An, J., Cho, S.: Variational autoencoder based anomaly detection using reconstruction probability. Spec. Lect. IE **2**(1), 1–18 (2015)
3. Antoniou, A., Storkey, A., Edwards, H.: Data augmentation generative adversarial networks. arXiv preprint arXiv:1711.04340 (2017)
4. Bao, W., Yue, J., Rao, Y.: A deep learning framework for financial time series using stacked autoencoders and long-short term memory. PLoS ONE **12**(7) (2017)
5. Barker, I.: Attack traffic up 32 percent in 2018 (2018). https://betanews.com/2019/03/05/attack-traffic-increase/
6. Bencsáth, B., Pék, G., Buttyán, L., Felegyhazi, M.: The cousins of Stuxnet: Duqu, Flame, and Gauss. Future Internet **4**(4), 971–1003 (2012)

7. Bencsáth, B., Pék, G., Buttyán, L., Félegyházi, M.: Duqu: analysis, detection, and lessons learned. In: ACM European Workshop on System Security (EuroSec), vol. 2012 (2012)
8. Bohara, A., Thakore, U., Sanders, W.H.: Intrusion detection in enterprise systems by combining and clustering diverse monitor data. In: Proceedings of the Symposium and Bootcamp on the Science of Security, pp. 7–16. ACM (2016)
9. Borghesi, A., Bartolini, A., Lombardi, M., Milano, M., Benini, L.: A semisupervised autoencoder-based approach for anomaly detection in high performance computing systems. Eng. Appl. Artif. Intell. **85**, 634–644 (2019)
10. Cappers, B.C., van Wijk, J.J.: Understanding the context of network traffic alerts. In: 2016 IEEE Symposium on Visualization for Cyber Security (VizSec), pp. 1–8. IEEE (2016)
11. Chandola, V., Banerjee, A., Kumar, V.: Anomaly detection: a survey. ACM Comput. Surv. (CSUR) **41**(3), 15 (2009)
12. Chen, T.M., Abu-Nimeh, S.: Lessons from Stuxnet. Computer **44**(4), 91–93 (2011)
13. Chhajed, S.: Learning ELK Stack. Packt Publishing Ltd., Birmingham (2015)
14. Chowdhary, A., Sengupta, S., Huang, D., Kambhampati, S.: Markov game modeling of moving target defense for strategic detection of threats in cloud networks. In: AAAI Workshop on Artificial Intelligence for Cyber-Security (2018)
15. Chung, C.J., Khatkar, P., Xing, T., Lee, J., Huang, D.: NICE: network intrusion detection and countermeasure selection in virtual network systems. IEEE Trans. Dependable Secure Comput. **10**(4), 198–211 (2013)
16. CSE-CIC-IDS2018: A collaborative project between the communications security establishment (CSE) and the Canadian institute for cybersecurity (CIC) (2018). https://www.unb.ca/cic/datasets/ids-2018.html
17. Cunningham, R.K., et al.: Evaluating intrusion detection systems without attacking your friends: the 1998 DARPA intrusion detection evaluation. Technical report, Massachusetts Institute of Technology Lexington, Lincoln Laboratory (1999)
18. DARPA: DARPA scalable network monitoring (SNM) program traffic (11/03/2009 to 11/12/2009) (2012). 10.23721/111/1354735
19. Davis, J., Goadrich, M.: The relationship between precision-recall and roc curves. In: Proceedings of the 23rd International Conference on Machine Learning, pp. 233–240 (2006)
20. Dhanabal, L., Shantharajah, S.: A study on NSL-KDD dataset for intrusion detection system based on classification algorithms. Int. J. Adv. Res. Comput. Commun. Eng. **4**(6), 446–452 (2015)
21. Dragon, D.: Double Dragon: APT41, a dual espionage and cyber crime operation. https://content.fireeye.com/apt-41/rpt-apt41. Accessed 29 July 2020
22. Du, M., Li, F., Zheng, G., Srikumar, V.: DeepLog: anomaly detection and diagnosis from system logs through deep learning. In: Proceedings of the 2017 ACM SIGSAC Conference on Computer and Communications Security, pp. 1285–1298. ACM (2017)
23. DVWA, U.: Damn vulnerable web application (2020). http://www.dvwa.co.uk/
24. Emmott, A.F., Das, S., Dietterich, T., Fern, A., Wong, W.K.: Systematic construction of anomaly detection benchmarks from real data. In: Proceedings of the ACM SIGKDD Workshop on Outlier Detection and Description, pp. 16–21 (2013)
25. Fontugne, R., Borgnat, P., Abry, P., Fukuda, K.: MAWILaB: combining diverse anomaly detectors for automated anomaly labeling and performance benchmarking. In: Proceedings of the 6th International COnference, p. 8. ACM (2010)
26. Ghafir, I., et al.: Detection of advanced persistent threat using machine-learning correlation analysis. Future Gener. Comput. Syst. **89**, 349–359 (2018)

27. Jain, N., Olmo, A., Sengupta, S., Manikonda, L., Kambhampati, S.: Imperfect ima-GANation: implications of GANs exacerbating biases on facial data augmentation and snapchat selfie lenses. arXiv preprint arXiv:2001.09528 (2020)
28. Kim, H., Kim, J., Kim, I., Chung, T.M.: Behavior-based anomaly detection on big data (2015)
29. Kissel, R.: Glossary of Key Information Security Terms. Diane Publishing, Darby (2011)
30. Kumar, R.S.S., Wicker, A., Swann, M.: Practical machine learning for cloud intrusion detection: challenges and the way forward. arXiv preprint arXiv:1709.07095 (2017)
31. Marchetti, M., Pierazzi, F., Colajanni, M., Guido, A.: Analysis of high volumes of network traffic for advanced persistent threat detection. Comput. Netw. **109**, 127–141 (2016)
32. Marchetti, M., Pierazzi, F., Guido, A., Colajanni, M.: Countering advanced persistent threats through security intelligence and big data analytics. In: 2016 8th International Conference on Cyber Conflict (CyCon), pp. 243–261. IEEE (2016)
33. Merkel, D.: Docker: lightweight Linux containers for consistent development and deployment. Linux J. **2014**(239), 2 (2014)
34. Micro, T.: Advanced persistent threat awareness (2018). https://www.trendmicro.it/media/misc/apt-survey-report-en.pdf
35. Microsoft: One-class support vector machine (2019). https://docs.microsoft.com/en-us/azure/machine-learning/studio-module-reference/one-class-support-vector-machine
36. Milajerdi, S.M., Gjomemo, R., Eshete, B., Sekar, R., Venkatakrishnan, V.: HOLMES: real-time apt detection through correlation of suspicious information flows. arXiv preprint arXiv:1810.01594 (2018)
37. Moustafa, N., Slay, J.: UNSW-NB15: a comprehensive data set for network intrusion detection systems (UNSW-NB15 network data set). In: 2015 Military Communications and Information Systems Conference (MilCIS), pp. 1–6. IEEE (2015)
38. Myneni, S., Chowdhary, A.: Apt dataset detailed description, March 2020. https://gitlab.thothlab.org/Advanced-Persistent-Threat/apt-2020/
39. OWASP: OWASP Mutillidae 2 project (2020). https://wiki.owasp.org/index.php/
40. Pang, G., Hengel, A.v.d., Shen, C.: Weakly-supervised deep anomaly detection with pairwise relation learning. arXiv preprint arXiv:1910.13601 (2019)
41. Qu, Z., Su, L., Wang, X., Zheng, S., Song, X., Song, X.: A unsupervised learning method of anomaly detection using GRU. In: 2018 IEEE International Conference on Big Data and Smart Computing (BigComp), pp. 685–688. IEEE (2018)
42. Roesch, M., et al.: Snort: lightweight intrusion detection for networks. In: LISA, vol. 99, pp. 229–238 (1999)
43. Security, O.: Metasploitable unleashed (2020). https://www.offensive-security.com/metasploit-unleashed/requirements/
44. Sengupta, S., Chowdhary, A., Huang, D., Kambhampati, S.: General sum Markov games for strategic detection of advanced persistent threats using moving target defense in cloud networks. In: Alpcan, T., Vorobeychik, Y., Baras, J.S., Dán, G. (eds.) GameSec 2019. LNCS, vol. 11836, pp. 492–512. Springer, Cham (2019). https://doi.org/10.1007/978-3-030-32430-8_29
45. Sharafaldin, I., Habibi Lashkari, A., Ghorbani, A.A.: A detailed analysis of the CICIDS2017 data set. In: Mori, P., Furnell, S., Camp, O. (eds.) ICISSP 2018. CCIS, vol. 977, pp. 172–188. Springer, Cham (2019). https://doi.org/10.1007/978-3-030-25109-3_9

46. Shiravi, A., Shiravi, H., Tavallaee, M., Ghorbani, A.A.: Toward developing a systematic approach to generate benchmark datasets for intrusion detection. Comput. Secur. **31**(3), 357–374 (2012)
47. Siddiqui, S., Khan, M.S., Ferens, K., Kinsner, W.: Detecting advanced persistent threats using fractal dimension based machine learning classification. In: Proceedings of the 2016 ACM on International Workshop on Security And Privacy Analytics, pp. 64–69. ACM (2016)
48. Singh, S., Sharma, P.K., Moon, S.Y., Moon, D., Park, J.H.: A comprehensive study on apt attacks and countermeasures for future networks and communications: challenges and solutions. J. Supercomputing **75**, 1–32 (2016)
49. Vincent, P., Larochelle, H., Lajoie, I., Bengio, Y., Manzagol, P.A.: Stacked denoising autoencoders: learning useful representations in a deep network with a local denoising criterion. J. Mach. Learn. Res. **11**, 3371–3408 (2010)
50. Vulnhub: Vulnhub Badstore (2020). https://www.vulnhub.com/entry/badstore-123,41/
51. Wagner, R., Fredrikson, M., Garlan, D.: An advanced persistent threat exemplar. MONTH (2017)
52. Wang, Y., Cai, W.D., Wei, P.C.: A deep learning approach for detecting malicious JavaScript code. Secur. Commun. Netw. **9**(11), 1520–1534 (2016)
53. Yuan, X.: PhD forum: deep learning-based real-time malware detection with multi-stage analysis. In: 2017 IEEE International Conference on Smart Computing (SMARTCOMP), pp. 1–2. IEEE (2017)
54. Zhao, G., Xu, K., Xu, L., Wu, B.: Detecting APT malware infections based on malicious DNS and traffic analysis. IEEE Access **3**, 1132–1142 (2015)

Author Index

Printed in the United States
By Bookmasters